The Films of Eddie Murphy

The Films of Eddie Murphy:

An Unofficial Look At America's Favorite Comedian From 48 Hrs. to Beverly Hills Cop: Axel F

by Mat Bradley-Tschirgi

BearManor Media

2025

Published in the United States of America by:

BearManor Media

1317 Edgewater Dr. #110
Orlando, FL 32804

bearmanormedia.com

Printed in the United States.

Typesetting and layout by PKJ Passion Global

ISBN–979-8-88771-735-7

Contents

Acknowledgements

I wanted to give special thanks to my wife Evanna Bradley-Tschirgi for listening to me ramble about Eddie Murphy at any opportunity during the past year while I was hard at work on this book. Also of mention are Walter Chaw, Jade Greenberg, Alison Macor, and Frank Santopadre for agreeing to be interviewed for this book. Last but not least is Johans Court who did an amazing job on the illustration for the cover of this book. A final shout-out goes to my colleagues at the Clubhouse rooms Writers on the Storm, Writer Roommates, and the Broom Closet who provided advice, humor, and support during the many hours I spent writing this book. Thanks to E.G. Fahie and Meg for providing feedback on early drafts. And thanks to you, the reader, for actually reading the acknowledgements section!

Introduction

In the 1980s, you could walk into anyone's house and, if they had a VCR, it was likely they had an Eddie Murphy movie or two. Odds are good it was *Beverly Hills Cop* (1984).

My first experience with Eddie Murphy wasn't with an obscure flick. Instead, it was one we saw in the small embassy theater in Buenos Aires, Argentina. I would have been in 2nd grade at the time. The movie was rated R, but Dad didn't care much about what we were watching as long as we saw it with the whole family. Whether he did this because we were mature enough or because he was just sick and tired of renting National Geographic specials and Disney animated features (we only owned a handful of VHS at the time, among them *Pinocchio* (1940), *Popeye the Sailor Meets Ali Baba's Forty Thieves* (1937), and *Sleeping Beauty* (1959)), I'm not quite sure.

Dad, Mom, my sister, and I sat in the theater to see what would be my first of many Eddie Murphy films: *Coming to America* (1988). I was an American living in a foreign country (my third in eight years); Dad's job required us to live overseas and move every two years to a different locale. Despite having never been to New York City at the time, I related to Eddie Murphy's character Prince Akeem feeling like a fish out of water in Queens. I knew what it was like to be a stranger in a strange land.

Being only eight years old, I laughed the hardest at the McDowell's jokes ("McDonald's has the Big Mac, we have the Big Mick. Totally different!"). If there was one thing I understood as a kid, it was McDonald's. It always tasted the same whether in the States or abroad, a rare constant in my life.

As I grew up, Eddie Murphy continued to release movies. Before too long, we had moved back to the United States. After a few years in the metro DC area in Centreville, Virginia, Dad got a new job working for Coca-Cola and we all moved down to Atlanta, Georgia. Another new city, another fresh start. Another place with no friends.

Before we moved into a house, we stayed at a Residence Inn. It was furnished temporary lodging somewhere closer to a townhouse than an apartment. We had stopped at a Blockbuster Video to rent two Eddie Murphy comedies: *48 Hrs.* (1982) and *Beverly Hills Cop*. Now 11 years of age, I understood more of the jokes. I recognized "Roxanne" by The Police and laughed at Eddie's falsetto take on Sting's vocals.

A few years later, my very first CD would be the soundtrack to an Eddie Murphy movie that would become one of my favorite movies period, *Beverly Hills Cop*. A ravishing mix of R&B and New Wave, the album had one song that spoke to me in particular, Patti LaBelle's "Stir It Up." In a life that to that point had been filled with uncertainty with all the moving (after moving to Georgia, I would end up living there for 14 years), LaBelle singing about holding onto pressure, packing up her clothes, and needing to stir it up spoke to me deeply.

Perhaps these early encounters with Eddie Murphy films and soundtracks inspired me to write this book. Perhaps they had nothing to do with it. As you peruse these pages, perhaps you can come to your own conclusions.

For those looking for full-color photographs of your favorite Eddie Murphy movies in this book, you'll have to look elsewhere. My research into getting the rights for stills from his movies quickly proved that such a thing would be too expensive for my purposes. In one case, I was more or less told "Unless you know Eddie Murphy, which you certainly do not, no photos from this film will be made available to you!"

This is also true of the challenges I faced getting interviews with actors and directors involved with Eddie Murphy's films. My attempts to reach out to them ended in rejection or, more commonly, emails that got nary a response. However, I did manage to interview film critics and professional authors about their thoughts on Eddie Murphy films and what makes him so memorable. I hope these interviews elucidate points which I could not. Many even came up with approaches to Eddie's work that would never have crossed my mind.

This book does not need to be read in a linear fashion. I organized my write-ups on the movies in four sections: *The Franchise Gems* (Eddie's movies that had sequels), *The Hidden Gems* (Eddie's best standalone films), *The So-So Gems* (Eddie at his most mediocre), and *The Not-So Gems* (the worst of the worst of Eddie Murphy's filmography).

Technically, I had to include two entries that weren't films. One was the pilot for the Beverly Hills Cop TV show that never aired; a version with French subtitles popped up on YouTube and was too intriguing to resist. The other is Eddie Murphy's first stand-up comedy special, *Eddie Murphy Delirious* (1983), which originally aired on HBO.

Read about the movies in any order you please. Each chapter on a movie has the same selection of credits followed by the tagline on the poster; in the rare case where there wasn't a tagline on the US movie poster, I translated one from a foreign poster or, in the case of the Beverly Hills Cop TV pilot where there were no marketing materials I could find, I used an amusing line of dialogue from the show. In the Making Of sections, I picked excerpts from interviews I found in my copious research that brings to life interesting factoids about the movies. In the Review section, I wrote a new review of the film exclusive to this book.

May this book entertain, inform, and encourage you, dearest reader, to watch an Eddie Murphy movie you may have missed or revisit one you may have enjoyed. Perhaps you'll find a new favorite. After watching all of them over the course of a few months, I can assure you that none are a total waste of time.

Mat Bradley-Tschirgi, September 6, 2024

Before the Films

Eddie Murphy knew he wanted to be famous at a young age. He had certainly been through his share of tribulations. After his parents divorced when he was young, his father was murdered by an ex-girlfriend. His mother fell sick, so both Eddie and his older brother Charlie had to live in a foster home for a spell.

While at the foster home, Eddie was described as a sweet boy who would watch and imitate people on the TV. He would point at the television and say, "I'm going to be on there someday!" After his mother healed, she was able to take her boys back in and remarry. Eddie's new stepdad had a nice job and provided a comfortable middle-class living. He even drove his new stepson to his first stand-up gigs when he was 14 years old. The Murphys were moving on up!

Despite being barely into his teens, Eddie Murphy's talent on the stage was apparent. His early stand-up gigs caught the attention of a producer for a show looking for a new cast: *Saturday Night Live*. After its first five years from 1975-1979, none of the original iconic cast remained. Chevy Chase was the first SNL cast member to ditch the show for a film career in Hollywood.and one by one, others left the show for (hopefully) more fame and more fortune. For the start of a new decade, 1980, *Saturday Night Live* needed a fresh start.

Producer Lorne Michaels was no longer on board. Nor was Al Franken, who was promised to be the heir apparent but didn't receive the honor. Instead, Jean Doumanian had the inevitable task of re-launching the show that had become "the reason you stayed in on Saturday nights." Its youngest cast member was Eddie Murphy, who by now was only 19 years old with the confidence of a man twice his age. In a first, Eddie Murphy was granted Featured Player status so the show could justify paying him less than the other cast members.

In short order, Eddie Murphy and Joe Piscopo became the biggest star talent of what had rebranded as *Saturday Night Live '80*. Much of the new cast, which included such future stars as Gilbert Gottfried (known for his signature screeching voice, Gottfried would later reteam with Eddie Murphy for a memorable scene in *Beverly Hills Cop II* (1987)), was sacked after *SNL*'s infamous 1980 season, but Murphy and Piscopo remained.

SNL is a hard show to make a mark on. Some comedians make a splash by imitating the latest celebrity or politician *du jour*. Others make signature characters with a grating catch phrase. On rare occasions, cast members will make a splash with short films or music videos. Young Eddie Murphy pulled a hat trick succeeding with all three.

Eddie's celebrity impersonations on *SNL* always had an absurdist twist whether it's the James Brown Hot Tub (Eddie yelps entering the hot tub that's too hot with the same vocal bursts James Brown spouts out onstage) or his Stevie Wonder singing "Ebony and Ivory" with Joe Piscopo's Frank Sinatra. Even at times stodgy stalwarts like Bill Cosby got the Murphy treatment with Cosby doing a commercial for (what else?) Lite Beer.

Eddie was no slouch in the original character department either. While these often had celebrity ties, they were so far removed from their source that they were really more original creations. The beloved green clay humanoid Gumby was turned into a kvetching Jewish agent in Eddie's comic hands. The avuncular Mr. Rogers turned into Mr. Robinson's Neighborhood urging children to scam their neighbors in delightful ways. His pimp Velvet Jones was a teacher of a different sort, letting the curious know how to be a ho.

Eddie Murphy's grandest moment on *SNL* might have been a short film from late in his run, "White Like Me." Going off the premise that he's being made up as a white man to see how much better treatment whites get from blacks, it's a fun take on the more sobering nonfiction classic *Black Like Me* by John Howard Griffin.

Speaking in a silly yet convincing patois, Eddie's white alter-ego is able to get everything from a good seat on the bus to the best loans at the bank with nary a problem at all. The kicker comes at the end where we saw a line of black actors and actresses getting made up as white people with the audience being told to watch our backs because we won't know who the real white people are.

Just a few years into his stint on *SNL*, Eddie Murphy got a movie deal to co-star with Nick Nolte in *48 Hrs.*, a police procedural for veteran writer-director Walter Hill. Creating in what many ways was the first buddy cop movie, *48 Hrs.* made Eddie Murphy a movie star with the way he played comedic and dramatic beats with ease.

After his first film became a huge hit in December of 1982, Eddie Murphy continued to appear on *SNL* albeit in a more limited capacity through the spring of 1984. As Murphy started to promote his films on the top talk shows like *The Tonight Show Starring Johnny Carson*, *The Dick Cavett Show*, and *Late Night with David Letterman*, he would bring on his Uncle Ray, one of the funnier members of Murphy's family. Eddie would sit back and laugh his ass off as his uncle would do one of his routines that was commonplace at the family dinner table on national TV. It was a nice way to give back to his family; later on in his career, he'd have his brother Charlie and stepbrother Vernon as writers on some of his films.

Now nearing its 50th anniversary, *SNL* continues to be an institution, but it might not have lasted past its 6th season in 1980 if it wasn't for Eddie Murphy's quick rise to fame on the show. Eddie Murphy had proved at a young age to conquer stand-up comedy and *Saturday Night Live*. His next goal was to be a big movie star, and *48 Hrs.* was a hearty step in the right direction.

Interview with Frank Santopadre

(Emmy-winning Television Writer, Podcaster)

How did *Saturday Night Live* play to Eddie Murphy's strengths?

He was a gifted mimic, a natural sketch performer, and he knew how to play to the camera, which is impressive for someone as young as he was at that particular time. Also, it should be pointed out that staff writers Barry Blaustein and David Sheffield helped a lot, writing memorable showcase skits for him.

What made him so intriguing as a stand-up comic?

Everything -- timing, stage presence, delivery, charisma.... I wish he did more of it.

Do you think Eddie might do stand-up again?

No idea if that's in his plans, but it might be nice to see him tackle the medium as an older performer and from a different perspective.

What are some of your favorite Eddie Murphy flicks?

I'm partial to some of the offbeat, less-known films like *Tower Heist* (2011), *Life* (1999), and especially, Steve Martin & Frank Oz' hilarious *Bowfinger* (1999). My personal favorite Murphy performance was in *Dolemite Is My Name* (2019), written by the ingenious Scott Alexander & Larry Karaszewski.

The Franchise Gems

48 Hrs.

(1982; Paramount Pictures) Director: Walter Hill; Producers: Lawrence Gordon, Joel Silver; Screenplay: Roger Spottiswoode, Walter Hill & Larry Gross, Steven E. De Souza; Cinematographer: Ric Waite; Editor: Freeman Davies, Mark Warner, Billy Weber; Music: James Horner; Cast: Denise Crosby, Brion James, David Patrick Kelly, Frank McRae, Eddie Murphy, Nick Nolte, Annette O'Toole, James Remar.

> *Nick Nolte is a cop. Eddie Murphy is a convict.*
> *They couldn't have liked each other less...*
> *They couldn't have needed each other more.*
> *And the last place they ever expected to be is on the same side.*
> *Even for... 48 Hrs.*

THE MAKING OF 48 HRS.

- "Nick makes you act. My first day on the set, I came off of *Saturday Night Live*. One Saturday, I'm doing something funny, then I'm on the set doing serious acting. [Our first scene], Nick came at me [pointing a gun] saying, 'Hammond, drop that gun...' I'm from comedy, so instead of being intense, I say, 'Hey, don't point that gun at me!', but he was so intense. We had to shoot the scene over and over again... He makes you get intense, he's so good! Nick's a real good actor." (Comedy n.d.) – Eddie Murphy (Actor)
- "48 Hrs. had been in development for most of the '70s. It had been rewritten 9 or 10 different times, never to anyone's complete satisfaction. And Larry Gordon's idea was to revise

it along the lines of being a black/white story. [Walter Hill] was about to do a draft when they found out [Richard Pryor] wouldn't be available. So he was sort of a little bit stalled. And then his girlfriend, who was an agent, said: 'I've got this client who you should maybe consider.' He was [Eddie Murphy], a young guy, never done a movie before, on *Saturday Night Live*." (Harris 2016) – Larry Gross (Screenwriter)

- "I came back from New York, I had met Eddie, he couldn't come to LA because he was so busy on the show, and I said to [Nick Nolte], 'Look, he's a great talent but he's not a trained actor so Nick buddy this is the way it's going to be, it's going to be like working with a little kid or a dog -- the one take that's good we're going to have to print it. So that means you have to be good every take!" (Guerrasio 2017) – Walter Hill (Writer/Director)

- "I had always kind of said to myself that I would never play a cop because it'd been done so much... I had always considered myself a little bit on the other side of the law, not like a criminal or anything, but driving down the freeway, I always thought they were after me, like we all do. I headed up to San Francisco to research detectives and the kind of men they are to kind of clear my own stereotypes and viewpoints of police officers; what are they really up to and what they do? I found men of great integrity, men who were really committed to a certain function in society of being a protector. Then, I was able to approach the role." (Archive n.d.) – Nick Nolte (Actor)

- "48 Hrs. is a comic fantasy, it could even be taken as a send-up of *Dirty Harry* (1971) that takes off because it's grounded in a clear-eyed notion of what makes people tick and what real life is all about, especially on the streets." (Thomas 1984)– *LA Times*

- "[Eddie Murphy's] engaging comic routine as a horny street hustler is incarcerated in an extremely routine piece of police work." (Ryan 1982)– *The Philadelphia Inquirer*

On its opening domestic box office weekend of December 10-12, 1982, *48 Hrs.* opened in 3rd place against some steep competition (Mojo n.d.). Ahead of it in 1st and 2nd place were 2 other comedies, the Richard Pryor and Jackie Gleason comedy *The Toy* (1982) and *Airplane II: The Sequel* (1982). *Airplane II: The Sequel* was the anticipated follow-up to *Airplane!* (1980), a popular spoof of the *Airport* quadrilogy (*Airport* (1970), *Airport 1975* (1974), *Airport '77* (1977), *The Concorde… Airport '79* (1979), which were increasingly loosely inspired by Arthur Hailey's novel *Airport*.

REVIEW

The buddy cop movie is a genre unto itself, and *48 Hrs.* is one of the earlier examples. You take oil and water and send them up against some hardened criminals. *48 Hrs.* is such an effective movie because of how much the leads clash with each other. They grow as characters and as friends by the end. Eddie Murphy and Nick Nolte on paper may seem like an odd pairing, but they do far more here than trade blows and quips.

After Albert Ganz (James Remar) kills Inspector Jack Cates' (Nick Nolte) partners, Cates gets Ganz' former accomplice Reggie Hammond (Eddie Murphy) out of jail for 48 hours to help track him down. Their case leads them to a country fried strip club and dangerous alleyways. Of course, they have shoot-outs and car chases every step along the way.

Feeling more like a 1970s film with how harsh it is in both tone and language, much of the comedy comes from how ageist and racist Nick Nolte's character is towards Eddie Murphy. They begrudgingly learn to respect each other towards the end, but the scenes with just the two of them yelling and/or smacking each other around are just as tense as any of the action scenes.

Nick Nolte (*Jefferson in Paris* (1995), *Return to Macon County* (1975)) is very intense playing a stressed-out cop, which works well against Eddie Murphy's more laid-back style. Eddie is often quieter here than his loudmouth persona in later movies, although we get a glimpse of Eddie Murphy's full charisma in the classic scene at Torchy's where he gives the redneck crowd a real piece of his mind. Despite their bickering, there's a real sense of melancholy at the end where Jack has to drop Reggie back off in prison to finish his sentence. That's no mean feat in a drama, let alone a comedy; *48 Hrs.* manages to work as both.

Walter Hill (*Bullet to the Head* (2012), *The Warriors* (1979)) shoots the hell out of the movie and makes every second of its lean

96-minute running time count. Ric Waite's (*A Time for Love* (1974), *Adventures in Babysitting* (1987)) cinematography has a nice grittiness to it that helps sell the stakes of the story. No scene feels truly safe, which makes the audience feel as under the gun as the characters in the movie do!

An efficient, and often riotous, procedural, *48 Hrs.* never overstays its welcome. It's a great first film for Eddie Murphy and a good preview of what a fantastic talent he'd grow into over time.

Interview with Walter Chaw

(Author, A Walter Hill Film: Tragedy and Masculinity in the Films of Walter Hill)

I really liked your visual essay "Profane and Profound" from the Netflix series *Voir* (2021) on how Eddie Murphy and his performance in *48 Hrs.* was a personal inspiration for you. How was the process of making that episode?

Oh, yeah! That was a real fun thing. It's a funny thing about that show. I kind of started out doing the special features for the upcoming at that time 4K physical release of *48 Hrs.* As I was going through with my team making that, the director on that piece mentioned that David Fincher was looking for some stuff for what became the Netflix series *Voir*. We pitched my concept to Fincher, and he was really open to it but a bit skeptical with it focusing so much on *48 Hrs.* I talked to him more about it, gave him the whole thing, and he was persuaded.

We did it a bit backward. We already had the piece completed, had a dry run of it. Julie, our editor, put some stuff together so we pretty much had it completed before we pitched it to Fincher. Luckily for us, he was open to go forward with it. It was sort of a pre-conceived piece.

In your episode of *Voir*, you stress the importance of the famous scene in *48 Hrs.* where, as my Dad likes to put it, Eddie Murphy walks in the country western bar like he owns the place. What was it like for Walter Hill directing that scene?

I think what it was about *48 Hrs.* in the first place is that Walter Hill originally wanted to work with Richard Pryor. Pryor decided instead of doing *48 Hrs.*, he was going to do *The Toy*, a movie where he's a literal toy for a white man. Walter ended up working with Eddie Murphy because he was dating this woman who would eventually become his wife, and she sort of was Eddie Murphy's manager. She said, "Here's the kid, he's on *Saturday Night Live*, he's sort of breaking big, we think, give him a shot!" So, he did and brought him on.

It was clear, I think, to Hill initially that this was Murphy's first movie. He was not comfortable entirely... They planned all the biggest scenes for later in the film. The screenwriter Larry Gross told me that the scene in Torchy's, the honky-tonk bar, was really touch and go. They weren't sure if they were going to keep it because it was so racially loaded, that they could turn off the Middle America audience off if they realized they were the ones the scene was talking about. They did know it was a big centerpiece scene and could definitely see Richard Pryor doing it because audiences were used to seeing that.

They kept that scene for the very end of the shoot. Early footage of Murphy was not good; he was getting blown off the screen by Nolte. Eddie really didn't know what he was doing in front of a movie camera. Even when the producers were viewing dailies, they were pressuring Walter Hill to dump Eddie Murphy from the movie and find somebody else to play the part.

Hill was pretty steadfast. He told the producers, "I see something in Murphy, you guys get off my set!" So, they held onto Murphy, let him ad-lib, and made him feel more and more comfortable. Pretty much the last scene they shot was the big giant scene in the bar. That scene became the big pivotal scene in *48 Hrs.* that people really talked about.

I think the success of that scene is what influenced *Beverly Hills Cop* for Martin Brest who also wanted a big showcase scene, which became the sequence in the restaurant where Eddie Murphy pretends like he's the lover of the bad guy, Victor Maitland's lover. I think we really saw that with a lot of other comedians in movies like Robin Williams where in 99% of his movies, there's a scene where just gets to riff and do his voices.

After *48 Hrs.*, Eddie Murphy was already being diluted in *Beverly Hills Cop*. He was being more audience pleasing and less threatening immediately. I think it's Murphy understanding he's a star and that he really could water down his persona a little bit. You see it in *Beverly Hills Cop* a bit, he's even more watered down in *Trading Places* (1983). There are some themes that are about race a bit, perhaps even controversial, but you see those less and less. *48 Hrs.* is a very aggressive film, and Eddie starts doing less and less of that all the way to more family films like his version of *The Nutty Professor* (1996), *The Haunted Mansion* (2003), stuff like that.

His comeback recently is *Dreamgirls* (2006) and *Dolemite Is My Name*, right? It's sort of like he's bringing back a little bit of the edginess that he began his career with. That's really how he got famous, and then he went Will Smith for a while.

For the sequel, Another 48 Hrs., it had a longer cut originally. When you spoke to Walter Hill for your book, did he have any good stories on that?

Yeah! Apparently, 45 minutes was cut out of the movie. Walter Hill couldn't really admit to it, I suspect there probably was a lawsuit with an NDA attached to it.

Brion James, the actor who played Leon in *Blade Runner* (1982), turns out to be the bad guy in *Another 48 Hrs.* (1990). In an interview, he talked about the footage that was cut out. He had a bigger role, he was in a lot more scenes. It was a real last-minute decision. They cut a ton out of it and sort of dumped it into theaters.

Another 48 Hrs. is a movie that Hill himself doesn't really own. He doesn't disown it, but he doesn't have a lot to say about it. It's maybe one of his most bitter films. That's a kind of funny thing to say about a guy who did *Southern Comfort* (1981), but it's nihilistic for no reason.

Really, what it feels like for me is that Eddie Murphy thinks he's too good for it. He's too big to act like his character Reggie anymore. Instead, he's going to act like Eddie Murphy. So, you have Nick Nolte playing Jack alongside Eddie Murphy being himself. You can see through the whole film, it's Walter Hill and Nick Nolte sort of smiling at Murphy making an ass of himself. Eddie's giving bad monologues to the mirror, he's struggling around with guns, he's acting like an action hero.

Murphy said in an interview once that *Another 48 Hrs.* was his fat and sad period. I think he really got very full of himself at that point. It's one of the only times to me that it feels like he did something just for the cash grab.

Is there an overlooked Eddie Murphy film that stands out for you?

Vampire in Brooklyn (1995) is a movie where he's powerful and sexy in it. He gives a more affected performance than in *Coming to America* where he plays a literal king. I think *Vampire in Brooklyn* really works, and I'm not sure why it didn't fly.

Angela Basset is great. What a cast! *Vampire in Brooklyn* is a real sleeper.

Another one I like is *Harlem Nights* (1989), although not as much as *Vampire in Brooklyn*.

Another 48 Hrs. (1990)

(1990, Paramount Pictures) Director: Walter Hill; Producers: Lawrence Gordon, Robert D. Wachs; Screenplay: John Fasano & Jeb Stuart, Larry Gross; Story: Fred Braughton; Based on Characters Created By: Roger Spottiswoode & Walter Hill, Larry Gross, Steven E. de Souza; Cinematographer: Matthew F. Leonetti; Editors: Donn Aron, Carmel Davies, Freeman A. Davies; Music: James Horner; Cast: Bernie Casey, Tisha Campbell, Brion James, Page Leong, Ted Markland, Eddie Murphy, Nick Nolte, Kevin Tighe.

The boys are back in town.

THE MAKING OF ANOTHER 48 HRS.

- "Ultimately, *Another 48 Hrs.* was my idea, and the story that we wrote was under an alias in the movie, because I wrote the story and I didn't want any more bullshit. If they would've seen "Story by Eddie Murphy" and Paramount just went through this big thing by Art Buchwald, it would've just given the critics something else smart and snide to say, so I went under an alias on the story credit." (SPIN 2020)– Eddie Murphy (Writer/Actor)
- "I'd try to shoot Nick's side before I shot Eddie's. Because Nick gets there in the morning and he's ready to go, like a horse ready to come out of the stall. Eddie stays up all night. He doesn't have as much sparkle in the mornings." (Thompson 1990) – Walter Hill (Writer/Director)
- "In the first [*48 Hrs.*], I [played a good guy], but in the second one, I became the bad guy again. I also do a lot of comedy and play good guys. I crossed over in a movie called

The Player (1992) as the studio head. After that, I could play both. I'm big and a lot of the stars are smaller, so, if you're big and mean-looking, you play bad guys. After *Blade Runner*, I was the meanest guy in Hollywood." (Tellado 1998) – Brion James (Actor)

- "The storm trooper mentality and behavior on Nolte's part that the film breezily takes for granted; if there's any irony about it, it's carefully designed to wash over the storm trooper types in the audience and not give offense to them--only to the rest of us." (Rosenbaum 1985) – *The Chicago Reader*

- "Murphy is loose and funny in a sequence where he's trying to cadge friends for money from a pay phone, and he has a rascally winsomeness that's almost Chaplinesque when he's being bullied by the behemoth inmate (Bernie Casey) to whom he's in hock." (Rainer 1990) – *LA Times*

On its opening domestic box office weekend of June 8-10, 1990, *Another 48 Hrs.* opened in 1st place (Mojo, Domestic 1990 Weekend 23 n.d.). There were no other new major studio releases out that week, although it beat out the sci-fi classics *Total Recall* (1990) and *Back to the Future Part III* (1990).

REVIEW

There's something tiring about even the title of *Another 48 Hrs.* that sounds like a burden. The gang is back together for a second round of crime-busting capers with director Walter Hill returning along with much of the cast of the original, but in many ways, this seems like a sequel nobody was asking for in the first place. It's hard to capture the magic of Eddie's debut. Even if *Another 48 Hrs.* were a masterpiece, it would never have the freshness of something completely new.

After completing his stint in prison, Reggie Hammond (Eddie Murphy) is once again recruited by Jack Cates (Nick Nolte) to help him with a big case. This time around, they have to bust the Iceman, a deadly drug dealer that's been dogging the force for years. Problem is, nobody's identified who the Iceman is. Reggie has a bounty on his head, and the clock is ticking.

Walter Hill really ups the violence in this film which gives the action scenes much higher stakes. A sequence where bikers attack a bus with cop killer guns is vibrant and dangerous as is the climactic shoot-out in a nightclub. While the comedy is not as good as in the first, the action in *Another 48 Hrs.* easily tops the original.

A large reason why this flick feels so slack is many of the scenes echo the original with a twist. The problem is, the twists are not as clever as what we watched in *48 Hrs.*, so it's nudging audiences to just give the first movie another go instead. In a way, it's the same problem *Beverly Hills Cop: Axel F* (2024) has with the case of one too many callbacks. Do it once or twice, it's cute. Any more than that, it's a nuisance.

Nolte is in decent shape here playing his cranky self to full tilt. It's too bad Murphy often seems bored by the whole proceedings, merely going through the motions. Even the gag of him singing along to James Brown's "I Got The Feelin'" on his Walkman in the bus is a pale imitation of him singing The Police's "Roxanne" from his jail cell in the first picture.

Although the plot twist involving the identity of the Iceman is a good one, the movie is trimmed down to such a lean running time (95 minutes) that there's no proper build-up to it. There's solid action in the third act, and Eddie Murphy gets to show off his Bruce Lee-inspired street fighting tactics, but it doesn't make up for the slog of the movie that came before.

Slow to start with a decent finish, *Another 48 Hrs.* is a poor movie no matter how you slice it. Although there are rumors of a third entry, possibly without Nolte involved, not everything needs to be a trilogy.

Beverly Hills Cop (1984)

(1984, Paramount Pictures) Director: Martin Brest; Producers: Jerry Bruckheimer, Don Simpson; Screenplay: Daniel Petrie Jr.; Story: Danilo Bach, Daniel Petrie Jr.; Cinematographer: Bruce Surtees; Editors: Arthur Coburn, Billy Weber; Music: Harold Faltermeyer; Cast: John Ashton, Steven Berkoff, Ronny Cox, Lisa Eilbacher, Gilbert R. Hill, Karen Mayo-Chandler, Eddie Murphy, Judge Reinhold.

He's been chased, thrown through a window, and arrested. Eddie Murphy is a Detroit cop on vacation in Beverly Hills.

THE MAKING OF BEVERLY HILLS COP

- "The impressions, and just... were making too much of [my laugh]. Even still! If you say do an impression, they'll do that laugh. They'll talk like me, and they'll talk like the Donkey from Shrek. If you say, do Eddie Murphy, they talk, 'Hey, how you doing! Hehhh, hehhh, hehhhh!' And it's like, that's not me!" (Dick 2024) – Eddie Murphy (Actor)
- "One of the reasons I originally didn't want to do it is because I had no sense of action. I thought, 'I can't do action, I don't know what action is, it doesn't interest me.' I'm not an action movie person. Guns and trucks and cars and crashes... You know, I told the producers, 'To a Jew, the only action is the stock market.'" (Fee33 n.d.) – Martin Brest (Director)
- "In the three previous scripts there was some humor, but they were more straight-ahead police thrillers. When you tell the plot of *Beverly Hills Cop*, it sounds like a police thriller and doesn't necessarily sound funny! Paramount

was surprised when they got my script, and it was much more comedic. They found it funny, and were surprised and pleased." (Rowlands 2012) – Daniel Petrie Jr. (Screenwriter)

- "When the movie producers were here [in Detroit], they filmed a lot of landmarks and things. When they were here doing that, [Gilbert R. Hill] kind of took them around town. They loved his tone and loved his attitude and they kinda gave him a little screen test [for the role of Inspector Todd]. The rest was history!" (WDIV n.d.) – Jason Colthorp (Detroit Local 4 News)

- "With Eddie Murphy, I did *Beverly Hills Cop*, *Beverly Hills Cop II*, and then another little film called *Imagine That* (2009) together. I love working with Eddie. There's something about working in a film where you know when you're doing it that this is going to be a blockbuster film. It just gives you such confidence, if you will." (Comics n.d.)– Ronny Cox (Actor)

- "[Beverly Hills Cop wasn't] a comedy when we started, it was an action movie for Sylvester Stallone. I was cast then Stallone dropped out to do *Cobra* (1986), so, I was in a movie with no star, then Eddie came on." (Melanie Brooks 2024) – Judge Reinhold (Actor)

- "Indeed, the movie's greatest pleasures arise from watching Murphy bluff his way into and out of various compromising situations, assuming a variety of fake identities with an uproariously reckless abandon that galvanizes his reputation as one of today's leading comic talents." (Ellis 1984) – *The Hollywood Reporter*

- "[Eddie Murphy] comes closer than ever to being able to carry a film single-handedly, although this one surrounds him with an excellent supporting cast. Mr. Brest displays a particular talent for positioning just the right actors in small roles and letting them make their marks succinctly." (Maslin 1984) – *The New York Times*

On its opening domestic box office weekend of December 7-19, 1984, *Beverly Hills Cop* opened in 1st place beating two new releases, neither of which were slouches (Mojo, Domestic 1984 Weekend 49 n.d.). The sci-fi sequel *2010: The Year We Make Contact* (1984) opened in 2nd place and *City Heat* (1984), a police procedural teaming up Clint Eastwood and Burt Reynolds, came in 3rd.

REVIEW

Eddie Murphy was on a hot streak after *48 Hrs.* It wasn't before too long that he did another movie that was a procedural like his first motion picture, except this time he was the lead: *Beverly Hills Cop*. A perfect vehicle for Eddie's talents, *Beverly Hills Cop* takes Martin Brest's gritty realist direction and pairs it with both laughs and James Bond-style action in one of the best comedies of all time.

After Mikey Tandino (James Russo) is murdered in cold blood, Detroit police detective Axel Foley (Eddie Murphy) tracks down the source of Tandino's stolen German bearer bonds... Beverly Hills. Helping Axel along the way are Sergeant John Taggart (John Ashton) and Detective Billy Rosewood (Judge Reinhold). The trio battle Victor Maitland (Steven Berkoff) in a climactic shoot-out at a posh mansion.

Comedic scenes often have a lived-in lackadaisical quality while the action scenes feel rougher than some might expect. Eddie Murphy is more confident here than he was in *48 Hrs.*, looking cool as he aims his firearm towards his next target.

In some ways, Axel Foley is a softer take on Reggie Hammond, his character from *48 Hrs.* He's a convict, not a cop, he mouths off in a more friendly manner, and he's oozing with confidence before he even enters the room.

Beverly Hills Cop boasts a strong supporting cast to boot, with Bronson Pinchot (*Blame It on the Bellboy* (1992), *True Romance* (1993)) nearly stealing away the entire film as Serge, an art gallery owner employee who enjoys making espressos with a lemon twist. Lisa Eilbacher (*10 to Midnight* (1983), *Never Say Die* (1988)) has nice chemistry with Eddie Murphy as his ex-girlfriend Jenny Summers while Steven Berkoff (*44 Inch Chest* (2009), *Rise of the Footsolider: Part II* (2015)) makes Victor Maitland into a credible threat as the villain. Berkoff is arguably better here in *Beverly Hills Cop* than he was playing a similar baddie in *Octopussy* (1983).

Another big reason for the film's success is the amazing soundtrack that features everything from Patti LaBelle to Vanity 6. Anchoring the upbeat tracks is an iconic earworm of a score by Harold Faltermeyer (*Cop Out* (2010), *The Running Man* (1987)). The lean 105-minute running time is buoyed by the slick sounds. *Beverly Hills Cop* is a lot of things, but it's never boring.

A buddy-cop procedural that manages to be moving (James Russo develops Mikey Tandino as Axel's old partner in crime so well that his murder is heartbreaking), hilarious (the strip club visit while Rosewood and Taggart are on duty is absurd in the best way possible), and action-packed (the shoot-out at the mansion would play just as well in a Bond picture), the original *Beverly Hills Cop* still stands as one of Eddie's best.

Beverly Hills Cop II (1987)

(1987, Paramount Pictures) Director: Tony Scott; Producers: Jerry Bruckheimer, Don Simpson; Screenplay: Larry Ferguson, Warren Skaaren; Story: Eddie Murphy & Robert D. Wachs; Based on Characters Created By: Danielo Bach, Daniel Petrie Jr.; Cinematographer: Jeffrey L. Kimball; Editors: Chris Lebenzon, Michael Tronick, Billy Weber; Music: Harold Faltermeyer; Cast: Alice Adair, John Ashton, Ronny Cox, Gilbert Gottfried, Eddie Murphy, Brigitte Nielsen, Jürgen Prochnow, Judge Reinhold.

Axel Foley is back.
Back where he doesn't belong!

THE MAKING OF BEVERLY HILLS COP II

- "There's a tension in the first movie that was funny about those guys chasing me, but there's something Musketeerish about the three of us getting together and solving a crime together!" (filmSCHOOLarchive n.d.) – Eddie Murphy (Actor)
- "One funny bit during editing was that Tony realized a mistake he made. We were watching the shoot-out scene where Ronny Cox gets shot, and we all realized we didn't have a matching shot to show who Ronny's shooter was. Tony looked at me and said: 'Oh shit, man. I've completely fucked up!' We had to go back and get that shot during pick-ups, but that was the sort of guy Tony was – it was controlled chaos all the time." (Clement 2020) – Billy Weber (Editor)
- "The way we did that scene with me and Eddie in *Beverly Hills Cop II* was all improv. I wish I had a tape of all the different versions we did! We were just playing off each other. One would say something, the other would answer

back. That was a lot of improv!" (Gilmore 2022) – Gilbert Gottfried (Actor)

- "I talked to Tony Scott about it, I thought we had to establish [my character] more, give him more shoots and more room. I didn't understand Hollywood at that time, and I ended up with less material than what was written for me originally!" (Arrose n.d.) – Jürgen Prochnow (Actor)
- "Tony's fascinated by the image and his own imagination. I'm very fond of the heist at the racetrack, and how Tony intercut the horses at the racetrack with the robbers." (steve6231 n.d.) – Judge Reinhold (Actor)
- "The film's style is that of a magician who keeps dazzling you with his right hand so you'll never notice what his left is up to." (Sheehan 1987) – *The Chicago Reader*
- "Cinematographer Jeffrey L. Kimball paints Los Angeles with the splashy gaudiness it deserves." (Howe 1987) – *The Washington Post*

On its opening domestic box office of May 22-25, 1987 on Memorial Day Weekend, *Beverly Hills Cop II* opened in 1st place, beating out the other two new releases of the weekend, *Ernest Goes to Camp* (1987) and the animated feature *The Chipmunk Adventure* (1987) (Mojo, Domestic 1987 Weekend 21 n.d.). *Ernest Goes to Camp* was based off Jim Varney's character Ernest, a character made popular in several TV commercials. *The Chipmunk Adventure*, a spin-off of the 1980s iteration of the long-running Chipmunk animated series which was birthed from a 1958 novelty record.

REVIEW

Tony Scott takes the helm for *Beverly Hills Cop II* from Martin Brest, and he couldn't be more different if he tried with his focus on flash and style. Eddie Murphy's take on Axel Foley is hardly the same either with his upgraded wardrobe and designer shades. A more commercial action-focused caper than the original, *Beverly Hills Cop II* goes all out in making it feel like a slick studio summer movie. It's still funny but less special than the original.

After Captain Bogomil (Ronny Cox) is wounded as part of a series of Alphabet Crimes, Axel Foley (Eddie Murphy) returns to Beverly Hills to investigate along with Detective Rosewood (Judge Reinhold) and Sergeant Taggart (John Ashton). They get tied up in an arms deal led by Maxwell Dent (Jürgen Prochnow) and Karla Fry (Brigitte Nielsen).

The increased budget for this film really shows. Tony Scott (*Days of Thunder* (1990), *Enemy of the State* (1998)) has shot a phenomenal-looking picture. In fact, the visuals are so distracting, it makes this movie seem like it takes place in a different Beverly Hills. Instead of being grounded in reality, this one often feels like it's in a fantasy land that's not so different from a James Bond movie. Action scenes and more frequent and violent, and the wisecracks are toned down.

The Alphabet Murders plot gives the plot more of a propulsion than the original. Eddie Murphy seems tired playing Axel Foley here as if he's more interested in his wardrobe and car than the hungry, scrappy cop from the first picture. The villains in this one are a touch more interesting, particularly Brigitte Nielsen (*Red Sonja* (1985), *Rocky IV* (1985)) as the ice-cold blonde Karla Fry.

Beverly Hills Cop II's comedic moments often feel a bit off with a few exceptions. Gilbert Gottfried (*Back By Midnight* (2004), *Silk Degrees* (1994)) is very funny as Maxwell Dent's accountant Sidney Bernstein, doing a give and take with Eddie Murphy in a scene that's shorter than an orange (or is it a tangerine?) wedge after Cesar Romero's put it through the ringer. Judge Reinhold gains an obsession for Sylvester Stallone and heavy weaponry which gives him a few bold moments during the action scenes.

There is no doubt *Beverly Hills Cop II* is a well-made film on a technical level, but it often feels like it's forgetting what made *Beverly Hills Cop* a sleeper hit in the first place. Everything from the soundtrack (Bob Seger's "Shakedown" feels awful milquetoast compared to Patti LaBelle's "New Attitude") to the cinematography feels too polished and safe. The explosions may be bigger, but the stakes feel smaller.

An above-average entry in Eddie Murphy's filmography, *Beverly Hills Cop II* could have tried a little harder to capture the magic of the original. This is a diamond that's no longer in the rough.

Interview with Alison Macor

(Author, Rewrite Man: The Life and Career of Screenwriter Warren Skaaren)

I loved how your book describes all the WGA arbitration Warren Skaaren had to do in his career as a screenwriter which included his work on *Beverly Hills Cop II* (the final Screenplay by credits read "Screenplay by Larry Ferguson and Warren Skaaren; Story by Eddie Murphy & Robert D. Wachs; Based on characters created by Danilo Bach and Daniel Petrie Jr."). Did you ever *read Fatal Subtraction: The Inside Story of Buchwald V. Paramount* by Pierce O'Donnell and Dennis McDougal about the famous lawsuit regarding writing credit for *Coming to America*?

I remember hearing about that case. It's just so incredibly complicated and things like that are still happening.

I understand why the WGA arbitration for screenwriting credits has to be there, but it's also such a stressful process for the writers. At the end, it seems like nobody is ever completely happy with the results...

Yeah, it can be soul-sucking. The fact that Larry Ferguson was pushing the WGA arbitration to get credit for *Beverly Hills Cop II* for so long... My book came out in 2017; I think I finished it in 2015 or so. I know I reached out to Ferguson, but I couldn't get to him.

I think I saw something relatively recently where he made some dismissive comment about that whole experience. I felt my blood pressure rising, took a quick breath, and told myself, "It's not my problem."

I managed to track down an early Larry Ferguson draft of *Beverly Hills Cop II* and it matched what you wrote about his descriptions of women mentioning things like their "swelling

breasts". While that was more common back then, such descriptors certainly aren't necessary for the story!

Right, and what Warren was trying to bring to the script was more dimension for all of the characters as well as the story. People still dismiss him and call him a hack, saying things like, "Oh, he really just came in at the end." Who knows what more he would have done with his career? I think Warren was always conscious of being, like, "Hey, this is a big blockbuster or whatever, but we can always make the characters interesting and a little more dimensional."

You frequently mention notes Warren Skaaren would write in the margins of his scripts, and they're full of sharp character-driven observations. Would you say focusing on character was part of his writing process?

I think it was. Warren didn't even go to the set of *Beverly Hills Cop II* because he was working on other projects. It wasn't the kind of personal immersion he had with his first big Hollywood movie, *Top Gun* (1986) [Warren ended up not getting any writing credit for *Top Gun* despite doing significant work on the screenplay, but he did receive an Associate Producer credit]. By the time he worked on Tim Burton's first *Batman* (1989) film, he had more of a stake in it in part because Burton wanted him on that London set. By *Beverly Hills Cop II*, Eddie Murphy was just starting to become the Eddie Murphy he is today in terms of his entourage. I think that some of that was taking shape, so I'm not sure Warren would have been able to directly reach Eddie on the set anyway.

I'm not sure why quite often Eddie Murphy doesn't get the respect he deserves. Almost every time he makes a movie, the press reports on it like "he's making a comeback!" when he's been making pretty much a movie a year for decades by now!

I was talking to my husband about doing this interview and trying to remember what would be my favorite Eddie Murphy movie. He reminded me how much we both love *Bowfinger*.

I was surprised to see how old it was, but it came out in 1999. I love that movie, and he worked so hard in that movie with the two parts. The interplay between him and Steve Martin was funny and complex.

When I ask people what their favorite Eddie Murphy movie is, the answer is usually *Bowfinger*. The movie did OK, it was profitable, but not as much as you might expect given the star power of Murphy and Martin.

It would be interesting to see how *Bowfinger* performed on streaming during the pandemic!

Agreed! It always rented well when I worked at Blockbuster Video decades ago. Did you ever get into Eddie Murphy's albums when he was releasing music?

Oh my God, "Party All The Time" was on the radio ALL the time! I remember thinking, "What do I think of this guy as a musician?"

I was in high school in the early 1980s, so I remember what a huge deal he was on *Saturday Night Live*. For him to make *Beverly Hills Cop* and make that huge transition. He was explosive; he was a star very quickly!

Reading your book, it was fun to see how technology back in the 1980s made working on screenplays a more tedious process before the Internet really took off.

Right. I mention how Warren would work on so many scripts in Austin and have to fax or mail them over to the directors he was working with, who were in LA. He used FedEx so much that he reached out to them to work out a deal where he would promote their services in exchange for a discount. He was very interested in technology and wanted to use the latest and greatest.

Do you think he might have preferred using a computer to write screenplays over a typewriter?

I think he appreciated the freedom it gave him. When he was working on *Batman*, he had to get a very specific computer that would work in Europe. When I talked to the archivist at the Harry Ransom Center at the University of Texas here in Austin, where Skaaren's archive is, they showed me different versions of Macintosh computers they had to buy to be able to read all the different versions of the scripts he wrote and kept on his computers over the years. He always had the latest model.

Beverly Hills Cop III (1994)

(1994, Paramount Pictures) Director: John Landis; Producers: Mace Neufeld, Robert Rehme; Screenplay: Steven E. de Souza; Based on Characters Created By: Danil Bach, Daniel Petrie Jr.; Cinematographer: Mac Ahlberg; Editor: Dale Beldin; Music: Nile Rodgers; Cast: Timothy Carhart, Hector Elizondo, Lindsey Ginter, Gilbert R. Hill, Eddie Murphy, Theresa Randle, Judge Reinhold.

In for the ride of his life.

THE MAKING OF BEVERLY HILLS COP III

- "We had to work out for a little bit because the movie is a lot more physical. That's because of Stallone and Van Damme and those guys are doing those wild action movies. Now, to do action, I gotta work out!" (Entertainment n.d.) – Eddie Murphy (Actor)
- "Three days in, I said to Eddie, 'Eddie, why aren't you being funny? I mean, you know, Axel is a wise-ass.' He says, 'Axel's a grown-up now, he's a man now.' It turns out in that moment in time, there were big black leads doing action like Wesley Snipes, Sam Jackson, and Denzel doing these big action serious pictures, and Eddie wanted to do that." (Gill 2023) – John Landis (Director)
- "I go to John Landis to see what notes he wants to give me, and they are all only about the fictional Disney characters. There was a pig called Virginia Ham, I think that's kind of funny. He says, 'Call it Priscilla Pig!' I realized it's about ego. Landis did not want me to go work for a rival movie, so I couldn't go do *Die Hard 3* because I had to come up with new names for the people in the costumes!" (Joseph 2022) – Steven E. de Souza (Screenwriter)

- "We knew that [Eddie's stunt double] could grab the side, but I wanted him to slip and hold on with one arm and make it look like he almost couldn't make it. It was so spectacular, and we had three cameras on it. We didn't need to shoot that again!" (Mannes 1994) – Rick Avery (Stunt Coordinator)
- "[Serge] has graduated from an art gallery to a boutique selling personalized luxury weapons, which is a fair way of gauging how far the inspiration in this series has dropped." (Rainer, Movie Reviews: 911 for '90210' Cop 1994) – *The LA Times*
- "When a movie mostly requires [Eddie Murphy] to shoot off a gun he becomes just another action star, and another talent wasted in lazily miscalculated material." (Schickel 1994) – *Time Magazine*

Beverly Hills Cop III opened domestically on May 27-30, 1994 (Memorial Day Weekend, the same timeframe as *Beverly Hills Cop II* 7 years prior). Unfortunately, *Beverly Hills Cop III* opened in 3rd place (Mojo, Domestic 1994 Weekend 21 n.d.). In 1st and 2nd place that weekend were the live-action movie *The Flintstones* (1994), based on the animated TV series which ran from 1960-1966, and *Maverick* (1994), another film based off a TV series, albeit a live-action one that ran from 1957-1962.

REVIEW

Part of what made the original *Beverly Hills Cop* so fresh was that it, like many early Eddie Murphy movies, was a fish out of water scenario. His character Axel Foley was a hard-edged Detroit cop trying to solve a case in sunny, chic Beverly Hills. Each *Beverly Hills Cop* sequel becomes a bit harder to swallow once you realize that he comes back to Beverly Hills every time; it's not a new experience anymore! Nowhere is this more apparent than in *Beverly Hills Cop III* (1994) which takes place in Wonder World, a pastiche of Disneyland. Despite still having an R-rating, the whole premise and film seems awful soft and tired.

After Inspector Todd (Gil Hill) gets gunned down during a raid on a chop shop, Axel Foley (Eddie Murphy) notices a truck full of counterfeit bills that he traces back to (where else?) Beverly Hills. Working with Sergeant Billy Rosewood (Judge Reinhold) and Detective Jon Flint (Hector Elizondo), Axel investigates the corruption that lies beneath a happy theme park where "happiness is king".

Things get off to a promising start with an action-packed opening in Detroit that also throws in a musical number set to The Supremes' "Come See About Me". Unfortunately, after killing off Inspector Todd, the air goes out of the balloon. It takes a long time to send Axel Foley over to Wonder World, and once we do, the scope never feels big enough; all the rides come off as chintzy. John Landis does an impressive job creating a cast of unique animal characters with striking designs. Landis' choice of hiring Richard M. Sherman (*Chitty Chitty Bang Bang* (1968), *Mary Poppins* (1964)) and Robert B. Sherman (*The Jungle Book* (1967), *The Sword in the Stone* (1963)) to create a unique yet annoying theme song for Wonder World helps add an authenticity the park itself lacks.

The counterfeiting plot turns into a bit of a farce with the real currency being swapped out for Wonder World certificates, and there's a lot of Eddie Murphy getting shot at by security goons in industrial concrete corridors as he tries to catch the baddies in the act. There's a half-baked romantic subplot with Theresa Randle (*Jungle Fever* (1991), *Bad Boys for Life* (2020)) trying her best as Janice Perkins that never quite goes where it should. Timothy Carhart (*Red Rock West* (1993), *The Manhattan Project* (1986)) and John Saxon (*Enter the Dragon* (1973), *From Dusk Till Dawn* (1996)) are strong as the aggressive villains Ellis DeWald and Orrin Sanderson, respectively. Bronson Pinchot makes a brief if not welcome appearance as Serge who is selling guns that do triple duty work as a boombox and microwave.

Much of *Beverly Hills Cop III* feels like it's going through the motions. Axel Foley has been funnier in other movies, and the amusement park setting isn't satirical enough nor is the action kinetic enough to keep an audience's attention. One of the more rote movies in Eddie's career, *Beverly Hills Cop III* is a limping afterthought of a picture.

Beverly Hills Cop TV Pilot (2013)

(2013, CBS) Director: Barry Sonnenfeld; Producers: Jerry Bruckheimer, Marney Hochman, Eddie Murphy, Shawn Ryan; Teleplay: Shawn Ryan; Cinematographer: Karl Walter Lindenlaub; Editor: Amy M. Fleming; Music: Robert Duncan; Cast: David Denman, Brandon T. Jackson, Christine Lahti, Eddie Murphy, Kevin Pollak, Judge Reinhold, James Shanklin, Sheila Vand.

This Damn Machine Sells Caviar?

THE MAKING OF THE BEVERLY HILLS COP TV PILOT

- "What I'm trying to do with *Beverly Hills Cop* now is produce a TV show starring Axel Foley's son, and Axel is the chief of police now in Detroit. I'd do the pilot, show up here and there. None of the movie scripts were right; it was trying to force this premise." (Hiatt 2011) – Eddie Murphy (Actor)
- "I'll just say that I really loved that process. Barry Sonnenfeld, the wonderful director of *Men in Black* and *Get Shorty* and many other things, directed that pilot for us. I got to work with Eddie Murphy and write lines for him as Axel Foley. And ultimately, it's a tricky situation, because I don't know that I even know the full truth. I know that the pilot was one of the highest-testing pilots that Nielsen had ever tested. But there were some politics involved at the time between CBS and Paramount, [which] had the rights, and Sony, who was producing it." (Swann 2013) – Shawn Ryan (Writer/Producer)
- "Axel Foley's son, Aaron Foley, is from Detroit. He's raw, you know what I'm saying? He's young. He's a bad-ass just like Axel was. He wants to solve the cases. He's still a cop. You know what I mean?" (TheHumorMill n.d.) – Brandon T. Jackson (Actor)

REVIEW

The TV pilot for *Beverly Hills Cop* looks very slick. Directed by Barry Sonnenfeld (*Addams Family Values* (1993), *Nine Lives* (2016)), it opens a bit like the original movie with a serious scene before things feel a bit more like the movies. Eddie Murphy's back as Axel Foley for a few scenes, but he pops with so much charisma that it makes the concept of weekly solo exploits focusing on his son Aaron dead in the water.

After a coke deal in Detroit goes sideways, drug dealer Dante (B.J. Britt) and his girlfriend Renee (Meagan Tandy) get murdered. Fledgling cop Aaron Foley (Brandon T. Jackson) barely escapes with his life and learns Dante planned to move his operation to Los Angeles. Dante had tickets to a basketball game with his friend Ricky (Christopher Rodriguez Marquette), and Aaron flew down to Beverly Hills to investigate with a little help from his father, Axel Foley (Eddie Murphy). Accompanying Aaron on the investigation are Detectives Leila (Sheila Vand) and Brad (David Denman). Standing in Aaron's way from doing things off the book is the Beverly Hills Police Department's attorney Rodney Daloof (Kevin Pollak).

As one might guess, there are a lot of characters in this pilot. Arguably, this plot is too complicated because pilots have the burden of introducing a new roster of characters to audiences for the first time. There's the standard sort of shenanigans (Aaron breaks into a house to investigate for clues! Axel puts on a quasi-foppish accent to get better treatment at a hotel!) one might suspect, but the plot is darker and more procedural than one might expect from a spin-off of mostly light-hearted films. It feels like a cop show first and a comedy show second.

Kevin Pollak (*Grumpier Old Men* (1995), *Willow* (1988)) is very funny as Rodney, the attorney for the BHPD who's a real stickler for the rules. There are some fun moments with Sheila Vand (*The Rental* (2020), *XX* (2017)) and David Denman (*Beneath the Harvest*

Sky (2013), *The Equalizer 3* (2023)) as detectives who are essentially the new Taggart and Rosewood, respectively. A running gag involving a $500 jar of caviar in a vending machine is one of the better ones on display, which isn't saying much.

Brandon T. Jackson (*Trap City* (2021), *Tropic Thunder* (2008)) has the thankless role of having to fill Eddie Murphy's shoes by proxy, and he's just not up to the job. It doesn't help that he has to sell dramatic chops in the opening scene (he doesn't), and Eddie Murphy runs circles around him in the comedic scenes. Eddie Murphy reprising his role as Axel Foley in the pilot was going to be a huge draw for the series, but unfortunately, it's too much of one. You wish this was an Eddie Murphy-focused show, and this wasn't the kind of project Eddie was interested in doing at the time. The concept and prestige of peak TV in 2013 was very different than it is today when more film actors work in TV or streaming series.

An amiable start to what should have been something special, the pilot for *Beverly Hills Cop* ends up wasting what could have been a solid concept. To add insult to injury, the final shot of the series has Aaron wear Axel's iconic Detroit Lions jacket on top of a white hoodie as a dubstep version of the Axel F theme blares on the soundtrack. Worth tracking down for only the most curious, this rare pilot is mostly forgettable.

Beverly Hills Cop: Axel F (2024)

(2024, Netflix) Director: Mark Molloy; Producers: Jerry Bruckheimer, Eddie Murphy, Chad Oman; Screenplay: Will Beall, Tom Gormican & Kevin Etten; Story: Will Beall; Based on Characters Created By: Danilo Bach, Daniel Petrie Jr.; Cinematographer: Eduard Grau; Editor: Dan Lebental; Music: Lorne Balfe; Cast: John Ashton, Kevin Bacon, Joseph Gordon-Levitt, Eddie Murphy, Taylour Paige, Bronson Pinchot, Judge Reinhold, Bee-Be Smith.

This Summer Axel Foley is Back.

THE MAKING OF BEVERLY HILLS COP: AXEL F

- "So, when I'm having somebody write something, it's always, 'Give me a solid story.' And, inevitably, they always go off and write goofy, funny stuff, and I'm like, 'No, no, no, no, no, no, no! Just give me story, story, story!" (Presents 2024) – Eddie Murphy (Actor/Producer)
- "The trick is to figure out a way to fulfill [the audiences'] expectations, and also some places to subvert them. So that was sort of the assignment. I think the 2018 *Halloween* [sequel] is a shining example of how to deliver a legacy sequel, and then I feel like *Top Gun: Maverick* is the best film to come out in 20 years." (Gonzalez 2024) – Will Beall (Screenwriter)
- "I want to make it modern and contemporary, but I want to go back really big, larger than life characters. These films, they were grounded! They were grounded and were honest and they were gritty too." (Erbland 2024) – Mark Molloy (Director)
- "It had to have the same concept of something simplistic because they're not big pieces. There are only six or eight instruments happening all the time, which is rare these days

and very difficult. You were restricted with the technology, so you couldn't have more than 16 instruments because he only had 16 tracks, so all of that was part of the respect of how to treat it." (S. Thompson 2024) – Lorne Balfe (Composer)

- "We had some nostalgia, but we cut some of it out... It was a little redundant, you know?" (Soto n.d.) – John Ashton (Actor)
- "In his strongest screen role in 2006's "Dreamgirls," Murphy won his first and still only Oscar nomination for playing a James Brown-like soul man who refused to fake his way to the top with a mellow sound that sells. Yet it's a mellow Axel F we see here, a father restored to love in his daughter's eyes." (Travers 2024) – ABC News
- "Murphy and two younger leads form an agreeable partnership in a good-natured romp that makes gallant, sometimes hilariously misguided, efforts to fit an eighties aesthetic around contemporary California." (Clarke 2024) – *The Irish Times*

Beverly Hills Cop: Axel F eschewed a theatrical release in favor of a direct to streaming release on Netflix. On its opening week of July 1-July 7, it clocked 41 million views on the streaming service (Seitz 2024).

REVIEW

Three decades after the release of *Beverly Hills Cop III* and fresh off the success of *Coming 2 America*, Eddie Murphy dives again into his well-worn well of characters to bring us back Axel Foley in *Beverly Hills Cop: Axel F*. A directorial feature debut from Aussie Mark Molloy, *Beverly Hills Cop: Axel F* often lays the hammer down on the nostalgia a bit too often to deliver a movie that rarely rises above understanding the assignment.

After learning from Billy Rosewood (Judge Reinhold) that his estranged daughter Jane Saunders (Taylour Paige) is in danger, Axel Foley (Eddie Murphy) once more ventures from Detroit to Beverly Hills to investigate a crime. At the heart of it all is a corrupt police force, but Axel has to figure out if his former partner Chief John Taggart (John Ashton) or the oily Captain Cade Grant (Kevin Bacon) is behind all the fracas.

The beginning of *Beverly Hills Cop: Axel F* is a lot to take in. Featuring three needle drops from the first two movies (including Bob Seger's "Shakedown", a fairly forgettable opening track from *Beverly Hills Cop II*), albeit with polished arrangements, this movie is at pains to remind you of the good old times the classic *Beverly Hills Cop* films delivered. After all these decades, it's a real shame the best screenwriters Will Beall (*Aquaman* (2018), *Gangster Squad* (2013)), Tom Gormican (*That Awkward Moment* (2014), *The Unbearable Weight of Massive Talent* (2022)), and Kevin Etten (*Kevin Can F**k Himself* (2021), *Son of Zorn* (2016)) could come up with is a tired crooked cops story that was old back when it was used for the plot of the second Dirty Harry feature *Magnum Force* (1973). Kevin Bacon (*Murder in the First* (1995), *Patriots Day* (2016)) practically blows the plot twist in his opening scene.

Much of the story focuses on Axel Foley reuniting with his new to the series daughter Jane Saunders, but this subplot is quite soapy and never carries the gravitas the cast wants us to think it does.

Sure, it's an acknowledgment that Eddie Murphy can pull off more subtle acting than he has in the past when a lot of his roles involved him shouting or acting surprised, but it feels like something out of another movie. Taylour Paige's (*High School Musical 3: Senior Year* (2008), *Mack & Rita* (2022)) muted performance does her no favors; it never feels like she earns the Foley surname.

Luis Guzmán (*Carlito's Way* (1993), *Dumb and Dumberer: When Harry Met Lloyd* (2003)) is quite funny in his brief role as karaoke drug lord Chalino Valdemoro. Bronson Pinchot makes a meal out of a small part as Serge, this time showing off a mansion belonging to the villain as a cover so Axel Foley can find out all the clues. Paul Reiser, John Ashton, and Judge Reinhold are largely wasted in retreads of their parts from the earlier pictures even if Ashton is given a bit more business to do than the others.

Joseph Gordon-Levitt (*Don Jon* (2013), *G.I. Joe: The Rise of Cobra* (2009)) portrays Detective Bobby Abbott as a well-meaning partner to Axel Foley who had a prior relationship with his daughter Jane. He has a lion's share of the dialogue to little avail. Both the 118-minute runtime and the action scenes add moments of great bloat to what should have been a leaner comic caper.

Coming to America (1988)

(1988, Paramount Pictures) Director: John Landis; Producers: George Folsey Jr., Robert D. Wachs; Screenplay: David Sheffield & Barry W. Blaustein; Story: Eddie Murphy; Cinematographer: Woody Omens; Editors: Malcolm Campbell, George Folsey Jr.; Music: Nile Rodgers; Cast: John Amos, Paul Bates, Vanessa Bell, Arsenio Hall, Sheila Johnson, Shari Headley, James Earl Jones, Eddie Murphy.

This summer, Prince Akeem discovers America.

THE MAKING OF COMING TO AMERICA

- "I was trying to come up with something to do that was really different, a piece where I was playing something other than Eddie, because I've been Eddie in most of my films." (Master n.d.) – Eddie Murphy (Actor)
- "*Coming to America* was the fastest movie ever made. From the day we finished principal photography, to the day it opened in 2,900 theaters, it was less than three weeks! By the way, it wasn't anyone's fault: we agreed to that release schedule. I was cutting negative and mixing and scoring during principal photography, and the picture was locked two days after filming ended." (Dursin n.d.) – John Landis (Director)
- "When, unbelievably, I was given this opportunity to design *Coming to America*, you couldn't find three yards of African fabric at boutiques in the United States; it was not the time. So, I went to my dealers in Brixton Market [in London]. I bought and ordered hundreds of yards of every different kind. You should have seen when that fabric arrived!" (BFI n.d.) – Deborah Nadoolman Landis (Costumer Designer)

- "Of the countless characters I've portrayed, King Jaffe Joffer remains one of the most enjoyable and iconic characters I've had the pleasure of playing. With his regal and commanding presence as the ruler of Zamunda, I reveled at bringing his presence to life for *Coming to America*." (Russian 2020) – James Earl Jones (Actor)
- " Rivaling the inept screenplay is John Landis' cornball direction, which includes a TV season's worth of reactive cutaways to an ugly poodle." (Byrge n.d.) – *The Hollywood Reporter*
- "Murphy is able to draw his black characters in a way that would have got a white man skinned alive, and not just in Africa." (Malcolm 1988) – *The Guardian*

On its opening domestic box office weekend of July 1-4, 1988, *Coming to America* was the only major new release of the weekend, knocking *Who Framed Roger Rabbit* (1988) back to 2nd place. July 1988 was quite a crowded summer at the movies, featuring such other hits as *Crocodile Dundee II* (1988), *Big* (1988), and *Rambo III* (1988).

REVIEW

Eddie Murphy's second film with John Landis takes an inverted take on Cinderella and applies it to the immigrant experience. A sort of riches to rags story, *Coming to America* broadened Eddie's appeal to become a smash hit around the world. A true classic, *Coming to America* is a promise of Eddie's greatness to be delivered in decades to come.

Upset with his arranged bride Imani Izzi (Vanessa Bell), Prince Akeem Joffer (Eddie Murphy) travels with his friend Semmi (Arsenio Hall) to find a better match in the New York City borough of Queens. After meeting Lisa (Shari Headley), Prince Akeem works at her father Cleo's (John Amos) fast food restaurant McDowell's to get to know her father better. Prince Akeem's father King Jaffe (James Earl Jones) finds out about this plan and is upset his son is trying to change years of family tradition.

Eddie Murphy plays Prince Akeem as someone raised from royalty sporting an African (Zamundan?) accent; it's not the same easygoing wheeler dealer Eddie Murphy persona he's largely played to date. *Coming to America* also marks the first movie where Eddie plays multiple characters in full prosthetics that are wildly different from each other (kvetching Saul, the Jewish barbershop regular, is a far cry from the preening Randy, lead singer of Sexual Chocolate); not unlike Peter Sellers, this is an approach to characters that Eddie Murphy really enjoys, and he goes back to it often in later films such as *Norbit* and *Vampire in Brooklyn*).

Arsenio Hall (*Blankman* (1994), *Sandy Wexler* (2017)) also does a lot of the heavy lifting in multiple supporting roles whether it's as Semmi, Akeem's well-meaning friend who sometimes gets in his way, the sanctimonious Reverend Brown, and others. James Earl Jones (*The Meteor Man* (1993), *The Sandlot* (1993)) gives a rich gravitas to the proceedings as the King, portraying a total opposite to the meek John Amos (*Let's Do It Again* (1975), *Touched By Love*

(1980)) as Cleo, the father of the woman Prince Akeem really wants to marry. Shari Headley (*Act Like You Love Me* (2013), *Goosebumps 2: Haunted Halloween* (2018)) is also solid as love interest Lisa who holds her own as a modern woman trying to figure out exactly what Prince Akeem and Semmi are truly up to.

Nile Rodgers' (*Blue Chips* (1994), *Earth Girls Are Easy* (1988)) score helps make Zamunda and Queens two distinct places while keeping a distinct 1980s synthesizer feel. Deborah Nadoolman Landis' costumes for Zamunda further make Zamunda feel like a real, lived-in country with its own culture, making the wardrobe a sort of character into itself. John Landis gives *Coming to America* a looser feel than *Trading Places* which works well given its more improvisational feel.

An early classic in Eddie Murphy's filmography, *Coming to America* has a sweetness to its satire that pays off in spades. A romantic comedy with both scope and stakes, *Coming to America* remains a genuine classic for a reason.

Coming 2 America (2021)

(2021, Amazon Studios) Director: Craig Brewer; Producers: Kevin Misher, Eddie Murphy; Screenplay: Kenya Barris, Barry W. Blaustein & David Sheffield; Story: Barry W. Blaustein & David Sheffield, Justin Kanew; Based on Characters Created By: Eddie Murphy; Cinematographer: Joe Williams; Editors: David S. Clark, Billy Fox, Debra Neil Fisher; Music: Jermaine Stegall; Cast: Jermaine Flower, Arsenio Hall, Shari Headley, Leslie Jones, Nomzamo Mbatha, Tracy Morgan, Eddie Murphy, Wesley Snipes.

A sequel is in the heir.

THE MAKING OF COMING 2 AMERICA

- "I was watching one of those *Terminator* movies with Schwarzenegger, and they used the special effect where they made him really young. I was like, 'If they did that, we could do a scene where we're young...', and that was the piece that made it all sort of fall into place." (Polowy 2021) – Eddie Murphy (Actor)
- "I was really inspired by *Fiddler on the Roof*. It's one of my favorite musicals, and I love the idea of a person who is entrenched in traditions for the right reasons suddenly realizing that the world is changing, and it's also affecting the people that he loves; mainly, his three daughters." (Singer 2021) – Craig Brewer (Director)
- "Let's do something similar to the spirit that Nile Rodgers had in that opening sequence where he used the chant over those trees, but let's do that on steroids! Let's have an orchestra. Let's have a harp. Let's have percussion. Let's have chanting. Let's have a choir. Let's have everything. Have it be

a celebration of the legacy of *Coming to America*!" (Audio n.d.) – Jermaine Stegall (Composer)

- "I wanted to bring something to the table to make it a little more fun. Imagine the kind of guy that you hate to love. He really means well. He's really a great guy. It's not his fault that he likes to play with grenades and Kalashnikovs." (Martinez 2021) – Wesley Snipes (Actor)

- "Everyone's here to have a good time with friends and cater to fan service, which isn't the worst way to spend two hours. Murphy and Arsenio Hall still gets laughs under latex as a barbershop quartet." (Simonpillai 2021) – *NOW Toronto*

- "How audiences will respond if they've never seen the original, directed by John Landis, is an open question. The 1988 film is referenced in almost every scene, although the paper-thin story isn't that hard to pick up on. Instead of using vintage scenes for flashback purposes Brewer and his team have "de-aged" Murphy and sidekick Arsenio Hall. How well this works is in the eye of the beholder." (Maltin 2021) – Leonard Maltin

Paramount Pictures eschewed a theatrical release for *Coming 2 America*. Instead, it made its premiere on Amazon Prime Video. Much like with other recent Eddie Murphy movies, it's frustrating to see *Coming 2 America* not get a major theatrical release, although that's more of a sign of the times and the COVID-19 pandemic than anything else.

REVIEW

The original *Coming to America* is a real classic that always seems to be part of someone's home video library; it's a comedy with a little something for everyone. To make a sequel to such a respected film is a challenge even Prince Akeem wouldn't attempt. Nevertheless, over three decades later, here we have *Coming 2 America*. A slightly softer PG-13 return to the land of Zamunda, *Coming 2 America* often feels like it's going through the motions despite some lively supporting performances that threaten to overtake the whole motion picture.

After King Jaffe Joffer (James Earl Jones) dies, Prince Akeem (Eddie Murphy) finds out he has a son born out of wedlock in Queens, New York. Akeem only has daughters in Zamunda, which is a problem because Zamundan law requires the crown to be passed down to the next male heir. If Akeem doesn't do this in time, General Izzi (Wesley Snipes) from the neighboring country Nexdoria (!!!) can usurp Zamunda's throne by forcing a marriage between his son Idi (Rotimi) and Akeem's oldest daughter Meeka (KiKi Layne). Akeem and Semmi (Arsenio Hall) fly to New York to retrieve his new-found son Lavelle (Jermaine Fowler) and return him and his extended family back to Zamunda. Waiting for Lavelle is a series of trials he must pass to become the next in line to the throne.

It goes without saying the plot of *Coming 2 America* has to jump through a lot of hoops to essentially repeat a lot of beats from the first film. The movie is loaded with so many cameos that it becomes almost as tiresome as *Deadpool & Wolverine* (2024). Any sequel is going to have elements of nostalgia in it, but when a movie is jamming so many past references down the viewer's throat, it can become an exercise in exhaustion.

The marketing for the movie feels a bit misleading. There is less going on in Queens here than one would expect. Most of the film takes place in Zamunda. In fact, by flipping most of the story to take place in Zamunda instead of Queens, this film resembles *Crocodile Dundee II* (1988) in more than a few ways. Sadly, this also robs the movie of its fish out of water qualities that made the original so fresh.

Jermaine Fowler (*Buffaloed* (2019), *Ricky Stanicky* (2024)) has the unenviable task of having to carry much of the picture playing Lavelle, Eddie Murphy's son, having to integrate into Zamundan society. His eagerness is nice, but both Eddie Murphy and many of the actors playing his family based out of Queens, which includes SNL alums Leslie Jones (*Christmas in Compton* (2012), *Ghostbusters* (2016)) as his mother and Tracy Morgan (*Head of State* (2003), *What Men Want* (2019)) as his uncle, often run circles around him.

KiKi Layne (*Native Son* (2019), *Don't Worry Darling* (2022)), Bella Murphy (*Dollface* (2019), *Fairyland* (2023)), and Akiley Love (*The Wonder Years* (2021)) do much better playing Akeem's daughters Meeka, Omma, and Tinashe, respectively. Their characters feel more lived-in and less cartoonish than Lavelle, and it goes a long way. Wesley Snipes (*Passenger 57* (1992), *The Art of War II: Betrayal* (2008)) is excellent as General Izzi, a feisty dictator who brightens up every scene he's in.

Eddie Murphy is less in this film than one would think, and it's to the movie's detriment. He gets some nice character work when talking to his children in the film, but there's a somber note to the performance that feels wrong compared to much of the comedy going on around him. A surprise plot twist at the end feels more corny than heartfelt.

Craig Brewer directs the film so it feels of a piece with the directing of John Landis in the original *Coming to America*. The entertaining dancing and musical sequences are often framed in wide shots, and there's a nice formality to the editing that makes the film feel more timeless than contemporary. It's a real shame that the movie is packed with too many characters and too much story, leading to an excessive 110-minute run-time.

A sort of stumbling sequel, *Coming 2 America* is pleasant enough but often feels like an epilogue rather than a true sequel. The PG-13 rating robs the film of the original's edge while some of the subplots feel more like something out of a soap opera than an out-and-out comedy. A fun watch for fans of the original, *Coming 2 America* should have been more special than it ends up being in the end.

Dr. Dolittle (1998)

(1998, 20th Century Fox) Director: Betty Thomas; Producers: David T. Friendly, John Davis, Joseph Singer; Screenplay: Nat Maudlin & Larry Levin; Based on The Stories By: Hugh Lofting; Cinematographer: Russell Boyd; Editor: Peter Teschner; Music: Richard Gibbs; Cast: Peter Boyle, Ossie Davis, Jenna Elfman, Gilbert Gottfried, Eddie Murphy, Oliver Platt, Jeffrey Tambor, Kristen Wilson.

Finally, a doctor who really gets his patients!

THE MAKING OF DR. DOLITTLE

- "[Director] Betty [Thomas] and I realized that instead of me going into the studio and finding 5 or 10 different voices for these animals, how about we find different actors, the right voice... Norm MacDonald's voice is perfect coming out of that dog! Chris Rock is perfect as a guinea pig! Garry Shandling is perfect as a bird, you know?" (take2markTV n.d.) – Eddie Murphy (Actor)
- "During this time we were filming, Fox in their inevitable wisdom put on a show *When Animals Attack*. Of course, Eddie'd watch that show, and then he would come in on Monday and say, 'Betty, I have this tape, you have to look at this! There's a kitty kat and they're attacking this man!'" (T. B. Archive 1998) – Betty Thomas (Director)
- "Aside from turning jolly-wolly British whimsy on its witty-bitty head by making Doc D a natty black San Francisco physician with a Cosby-perfect family (including actual Cosby alumna Raven-Symone), *Dr. Dolittle* upends Murphy's

usual position as a loose live wire by making him the reactive straight man to a bunch of winged and furry wisenheimers." (Schwarzbaum 1998) – *Entertainment Weekly*

- "The animals tear off some funny one-liners, and there's a nice little money-isn't-everything lesson." (Addiego June) – *San Francisco Examiner*

On its opening domestic box office weekend of June 26-28th, 1998, *Doctor Dolittle* opened in 1st place (Mojo, Domestic 1998 Weekend 26 n.d.). *Out of Sight* (1998), a thriller starring Jennifer Lopez and George Clooney, was the other major new release of the weekend opening in 4th place.

REVIEW

The original *Doctor Dolittle* (1967) live-action musical starring Rex Harrison featuring songs by Leslie Bricusse and Lionel Newman was a notorious flop. This 1998 Eddie Murphy take on the material takes almost nothing from the original film and novels by Hugh Lofting except for the title and a lovely cover of "Talk to the Animals" by Louis Armstrong that plays over the end credits. Despite its lack of fidelity to the source material, *Dr. Dolittle* is an amiable modern take on a doctor who speaks and squawks with the animals.

As a child, John Dolittle can talk to animals but manages to suppress his abilities after a traumatic incident where his parents hire a priest to exorcise him. As a middle-aged adult, Dolittle (Eddie Murphy) has become a doctor who works on humans until one day he nearly hits Lucky the Dog (Norm MacDonald), causing him to regain his powers back. Pretty soon, he starts building up a client list that's full of all sorts of critters. Dolittle manages to struggle balancing his family, human patients, and animal patients as zaniness ensues.

Much was made at the time of the CG used to make animals talk realistically; the special effects here are much more sophisticated than in something like *Mister Ed*. Even by modern standards, the special effects hold up quite well because they are pretty subtle for the most part. The decision to go with a variety of top comics as the voice of the different animals is very smart as it keeps the performances from being too flat and makes spotting every animal a game that keeps the audiences guessing as to which comedian will voice one next.

Norm MacDonald (*Hollywood & Wine* (2010), *Vampire Dog* (2012)) is especially strong as Lucky, a dog that uses Norm's trademark laconic passive-aggressive Canadian delivery to fantastic effect. Nat Maudlin (*A Christmas Story 2* (2012), *The Preacher's*

Wife (1996)) and Larry Levin's (*Bakersfield P.D.* (1993), *I Love You, Man* (2009)) screenplay has some strong one-liners such as when being given a rectal thermometer, Lucky the dog quips, "I'm going to swallow the thermometer, and I don't mean in my mouth!"

Although Eddie Murphy is kind of unremarkable in the lead (his choice to often underplay the good doctor makes him often fade into the background when all the animal hijinks are going on), the supporting cast is often strong. Jeffrey Tambor (*Hellboy II: The Golden Army* (2008), *Life Stinks* (1991)) is especially nice as the well-meaning yet officious veterinarian Dr. Fish.

Part of what works in this version of *Dr. Dolittle* is the comedy between the doctor trying to play it cool when he can understand and talk to animals without letting other humans know about his special skill set. This adds a bit of suspense to scenes that would be lost if everyone just knew he was a famous animal doctor.

Less effective is the treacly family drama with his daughter. So many of Eddie Murphy's comedies have subplots about an overworked father who realizes that what's really most important is spending time with your own family. It's a wholesome message but one that's all too well-trodden, and the spin on it here comes off as very cheesy.

A pretty good family comedy, *Dr. Dolittle* has its moments but never really aspires to greatness. It doesn't rise above mediocrity. *Dr. Dolittle* lacks a certain lagniappe.

Dr. Dolittle 2 (2001)

(2001, 20th Century Fox) Director: Steve Carr; Producers: John Davis, Joseph Singer; Screenplay: Larry Levin; Based on the Stories By: Hugh Lofting; Cinematographer: Daryn Okada; Editor: Craig Herring; Music: David Newman; Cast: James Avery, Jeffrey Jones, Norm MacDonald, Eddie Murphy, Andy Richter, Raven-Symoné, Kristen Wilson, Steve Zahn.

Dolittle is back.

THE MAKING OF DR. DOLITTLE 2

- "Our first *Dolittle* was about him realizing that he has this gift and how he comes to grips with it. Now that the world knows he can talk to animals, how is it going change his relationship with his family, and how is he going to use his special talents?" (Cinema.com n.d.) – Eddie Murphy (Actor)
- "I thought, I should take this because it has everything I don't want to work with -- a big star, animals, special effects. But I was this big idiot confident guy, and I told the studio that you could learn special effects, but you couldn't learn to be funny." (Staff 2001) – Steve Carr (Director)
- "Roger, the stand-in that Eddie is talking to, helps Eddie react well to where the bear is going to be and get a good eyeline. The bear is put in next [in a shot all by itself], and the trainer off to the side will have to be digitally removed." (Make-Up n.d.) – Doug Smith (Production Visual Effects Supervisor)
- "Despite a subversive sense of humor, *Dr. Dolittle 2* has its obligatory, perhaps even sincere, messages about respect for not only our own families but also the family of Mother Earth." (Kempley 2001) – *The Washington Post*

- "The best animal is a Latino lizard that thinks it can blend in with the environment, though it never changes from its green skin tone. Yeah, it's 'funny' for a second, but gets old and juvenile real fast." (Gore 2001) – *Film Threat*

On its opening box office weekend of June 22-24, 2001, *Dr. Dolittle 2* opened in 2nd place (Mojo, Domestic 2001 Weekend 25 n.d.). In 1st place was another newcomer and one that would be the start of a franchise of its own, *The Fast and the Furious* (2001). Over the next few years, there were three *Dr. Dolittle* direct-to-video sequels released not featuring Eddie Murphy: *Dr. Dolittle 3* (2006), *Dr. Dolittle: Tail to the Chief* (2008), and *Dr. Dolittle: Million Dollar Mutts* (2009).

REVIEW

After *Dr. Dolittle* became another Eddie Murphy family film success, *Dr. Dolittle 2* came along to yet again give a very loose take on the novels by Hugh Lofting. A truly unnecessary sequel, *Dr. Dolittle 2* trades the suburbs for a verdant forest setting where fart and anxiety jokes (sometimes in the same scene!) often ensue.

Dr. Dolittle (Eddie Murphy) is drawn into a forest fracas where the fate of the woods hangs in the balance. Unless he can get the rare Pacific western bears to mate, the forest goes kaput. Dolittle has to get ursine Archie (Steve Zahn) to clean up his slovenly ways so he can put the moves on fellow bear Ava (Lisa Kudrow).

There's really little here to entertain all but the tiniest of tots. The humor feels a bit cruder than in the first film, but the scenarios are also a bit more rote. It's not new that Dr. Dolittle can speak to the animals, and the quasi-romance angle is barely tolerable. The "save the forest" angle isn't a bad one and is truer to the spirit of the novels than Dolittle trying to help Archie get his groove back.

Steve Zahn (*Hamlet* (2000), *Tall Girl 2*)) has a fun slacker delivery as Archie the bear, and Norm Macdonald continues his steady sardonic work as Lucky the dog. Raven-Symoné (*College Road Trip* (2008), *The Princess Diaries 2: Royal Engagement* (2004)) gets a larger role to do here as she discovers she has her father's powers of communicating with furry friends. Lisa Kudrow (*Like a Boss* (2020), *Neighbors 2: Sorority Rising* (2016)) is alright as the romantic interest Ava. Even better is Jeffrey Jones (*The Pest* (1997), *Transylvania 6-5000* (1985)) as the evil head of Potter Wood Industries, hearkening back to his string of playing heavies in 1980s comedies.

Eddie Murphy seems a bit disengaged reprising Dr. Dolittle here. Any energy he had in the original has gone the way of the dodo. The first movie had some cute moments here and there, but most scenes in *Dr. Dolittle 2* feel just like old hat.

Uninspired and more than a little turgid, *Dr. Dolittle 2* does very little indeed. Staring at a cow pie would invoke more wonder than this odious motion picture.

The Haunted Mansion (2003)

(2003; Buena Vista Pictures) Director: Rob Minkoff; Producers: Andrew Gunn, Don Hahn; Screenplay: David Berenbaum; Cinematographer: Remi Adefarasin; Editor: Priscilla Nedd-Friendly; Music: Mark Mancina; Cast: Aree Davis, Marc John Jefferies, Eddie Murphy, Nathaniel Parker, Wallace Shawn, Terence Stamp, Marsha Thomason, Jennifer Tilly.

Check your pulse at the door... if you have one.

THE MAKING OF THE HAUNTED MANSION

- "That was the whole idea of [*The Haunted Mansion*], to take elements from the attraction at Disneyland and to add to it, bring it into the 21st century. There's so much more you can do now!" (101 n.d.) – Eddie Murphy (Actor)
- "Everyone had different ideas of what to do: make it scary, make it funny. Everybody has different ways they want to do it. We finally came up with a version that we thought worked, which is when we got Don Hahn and Rob involved." (Tuckey 2023) – David Berenbaum (Screenwriter)
- "You're working by yourself, and you're imagining all the things that are going on. You do the line over and over again until you get it to where you want it." (DVDXtras n.d.) – Jennifer Tilly (Actress)
- "There's a non-threatening storybook quality to the film that should go over well with the kids but may just bore parents to death." (E. Gonzalez 2003) – *Slant Magazine*
- "Neither frightening nor funny, Rob Minkoff's yawn-inducing comedy-horror may share *Pirates of the Caribbean's* basic premise, but isn't worthy to scrub the latter's galley floor." (Empire 2000) – *Empire Magazine*

The Haunted Mansion opened in 1st place at the domestic box office on Thanksgiving weekend in 2003. Other new films opening that weekend included a new Michael Crichton film (*Timeline* (2000)) and a Christmas-themed dark comedy that would become a comedy classic (*Bad Santa* (2000)). Twenty years later, Disney would take another stab at this theme park ride with *Haunted Mansion* (2023) starring Danny DeVito and Tiffany Haddish.

REVIEW

Disney has not been shy about making films based off their famous theme park attractions. Hot off the heels of *The Pirates of the Caribbean: The Curse of the Black Pearl* (2003) comes an obvious choice for a theme park movie, *The Haunted Mansion*. Eddie Murphy stars in a typical sort of role as a workaholic realtor who learns how valuable his family is when they go to try to sell a fancy mansion during what is supposed to be a family weekend. The catch, as one might guess from the title, is that it's haunted. Conveniently enough, there's a flood and his family is stuck there for the night.

Other than a moody opening credit sequence showing a hanging and a later scene involving zombies, *The Haunted Mansion* tends to stick to the lighter side of horror going for a friendly *Addams Family* vibe. Director Rob Minkoff (*Stuart Little* (1999), *The Lion King* (1994)) has elements from the ride in here (he can't seem to get enough of the singing stone busts for comical effect), but the choice to make it a contemporary story instead of an origin story for the ghosts makes the mansion setting not as effective as it could have been.

Eddie Murphy doesn't have a lot to work with given the role of Jim Evers. It can be funny when he imitates the voice of the arch Master Edward Gracey (Nathaniel Parker) or tells his son Michael (Marc John Jefferies) to "whack those spiders!" Too bad David Berenbaum's (*Elf* (2003), *Strange Magic* (2015)) screenplay is so focused on the angle of Jim reuniting with his family that Murphy never gets a chance to let loose with the comedic gifts everyone knows him for.

Some of the supporting parts can be fun. Jennifer Tilly (*Bound* (1996), *Bride of Chucky* (1998)) makes for a sarcastic Madame Leota, and Wallace Shawn (*The Princess Bride* (1987), *Rifkin's Festival* (2020)) is boisterous as the ghost Ezra. Nathaniel Parker (*Beverly Hills Ninja* (1997), *Stardust* (2007)) makes for a creepy obsessive villain in Master Edward Gracey, but it is the great Terence Stamp

(*Superman II* (1980), *The Limey* (1999)) who steals the show as the droll butler Ramsley, dropping bon mots with a deliberate wheeze.

The Haunted Mansion's slow build to the not that spooky goings-on is appreciated. An extended zombie sequence featuring a thrilling escape has great makeup and real dread the rest of the film could have benefited from. A reveal on the true cause of Gracey's wife's death at the climax is effective, but even that's cut short by the dopey final shot of the family driving away with the Singing Busts in tow.

The Haunted Mansion isn't a total loss. Spooky moments are helped by good special effects and massive sets. Without Eddie Murphy in the lead, this film would have hit its mark better. Here, he seems miscast in a role that defangs him of any comedic mileage one would expect by placing him in a house with grim, grinning ghosts. *The Haunted Mansion* could have been great; instead, it's merely good.

Mulan (1998)

(1996, Buena Vista Pictures Distribution) Directors: Tony Bancroft, Barry Cook; Producer: Pam Coats; Screenplay: Rita Hsiao & Chris Sanders, Philip LaZebnik & Raymond Singer, Eugenia Bostwick-Singer; Story: John Sanford, Chris Williams, Tim Hodge, Julius Aguimatang, Burny Mattinson, Lorna Cook, Barry Johnson, Thom Enriquez, Ed Gombert, Joe Grant, Floyd Norman; Additional Story Material: Linda Woolverton, Jodi Ann Johnson, Alan Ormsby, David Reynolds, Don Dougherty, Jorgen Klubien, Denis Rich, Joe Ekers, Theodore Newton, Larry Scholl, Daan Jippes, Frank Nissen, Jeff Snow; Editor: Michael Kelly; Music: Jerry Goldsmith; Cast: Miguel Ferrer, June Foray, James Hong, Pat Morita, Eddie Murphy, George Takei, Ming-Na Wen, B.D. Wong.

Going your own way requires great courage.

THE MAKING OF MULAN

- "Eddie's voice provided a lot to work with. He gave such a brilliant and hilarious reading that it challenged me to come up with something really worthy." (Korkis 2022) – Tom Bancroft (Supervising Animator)
- "Barry came from the effects department and used to be a painter while I came from clean-up and then animation. So, we split off the film based on departments and our skill sets. Barry was in charge of the layout, background and effect departments while I was in charge of CG animation, 2d animation and clean-up departments." (Manwaring 20185) – Tony Bancroft (Co-Director)
- "The relationship between Mulan and her father is the heart of this movie. It's one of the things that really sets it apart." (Červinka n.d.) – Mark Henn (Supervising Animator)

- "Back then, the whole idea of trying to cast the right ethnic actors for the right ethnic characters, I don't think it was in the back of most people's minds. So the fact that they really went out and looked for as many actors who were of Asian descent is as a real credit to them." (Bergren 2018) – Ming-Na Wen (Actress)
- "The script is mostly drum-tight and brimming with gags; there's even some amusing but sensitively illustrated play on the complexities of Oriental religious customs." (Adams 2014) – *Time Out*
- "Pop-conscious settings of five songs by composer Matthew Wilder and lyricist David Zippel are deftly integrated into the film." (Stack 1998) – *San Francisco Examiner*

On its opening domestic box office weekend, *Mulan* opened in 2nd place (Mojo, Domestic 1998 Weekend 25 n.d.). The other major new release that week which beat it in 1st place was *The X Files*, the first feature film spin-off of the popular TV series. Disney followed up *Mulan* with *Mulan II* (2004) as part of their trend of releasing tons of direct-to-DVD sequels to their animated classics at the time. In 2020, Disney released a live-action remake of *Mulan* that notably lacked Eddie Murphy's character of Mushu the dragon. It should be noted since Hua Mulan is a legendary piece of Chinese folklore, it has been adapted into films as early as 1927; there have also been other animated versions over the years.

REVIEW

Coming hot off the heels of a trio of Disney animated features that couldn't live up to the juggernaut status of *Beauty and the Beast* (1991), *Aladdin* (1992), and *The Lion King* (1994), *Mulan* had a lot to live up to. Thankfully, it succeeds for the most part, combining some heartfelt musical numbers with epic scenes of war, and every so often, some comedy that can feel out of place.

After Shan Yu (Miguel Ferrer) leads the Huns on increasingly aggressive attacks into China, the Emperor starts recruiting men to the Imperial Army. Not wanting her father to join, Mulan (Ming-Na Wen) disguises herself as a man and joins the army to repel the Hun horde. At her side is the guardian dragon Mushu (Eddie Murphy).

Although Disney features in the 1990s had tried to give female characters more active roles to mixed results (Esmeralda in *The Hunchback of Notre Dame* (1996) being a highlight), *Mulan* is the first to feature a female lead. Not only that, but the character of Mulan is also complex, drives the story forward, and has to disguise herself as a man to take an active part in the war against the Huns. Ming-Na Wen (*April Rain* (2014), *Street Fighter* (1994)) does a hell of a job voicing a very challenging part. B.D. Wong (*Father of the Bride Part II* (1995), *Heart of Stone* (2023)) also does well balancing comedic and dramatic beats.

Given that this is a Disney film, we have two animal companions jammed into the story. Of the two, Mulan's cricket Cri-Kee (Frank Welker) is the most egregious, often plopped into scenes to add an extra dash of cuteness to what is a most serious and somber tale. The dragon Mushu has funny one-liners here and there along with an energetic Eddie Murphy performance (clearly, Disney is looking for snappy comedic relief like Robin Williams' Genie in *Aladdin*), but, just like the Gargoyles in their animated feature of *The Hunchback of Notre Dame*, the character comes across as superfluous.

Music is kind of a mixed bag here apart from two numbers, which is a real shame. Originally, Alan Menken and Stephen Schwartz were set to reprise songwriting duties from *The Hunchback of Notre Dame*, but for various reasons Matthew Wilder and David Zippel were chosen instead. Mulan's ballad "Reflection" is truly a wonderful number, and Captain Li Shang's "Be a Man" has its strapping moments, but the rest of the soundtrack is largely forgettable outside of a moody Jerry Goldsmith score. Originally, *Mulan* was meant to have more songs, but these were wisely dropped.

Directors Barry Cook (*Arthur Christmas* (2011), *Walking with Dinosaurs: The Movie* (2013)) and Tony Bancroft (*Animal Crackers* (2017), *The Origin of Stitch* (2005)) do an especially good job with the battle scene near the end of the film showing an epic conflict with a real sense of danger not felt in a Disney film in quite some time. Its mixture of action and cast of Asian characters (often voiced by actors of Asian descent) in a Disney film still make it stand out today.

One of Disney's better animated feature efforts, *Mulan* holds up better than many other cartoon features from the late 1990s. Often showing a sense of grace and maturity, this one is worth a rewatch.

The Nutty Professor (1996)

(1996, Universal Pictures) Director: Tom Shadyac; Producers: Brian Grazer, Russell Simmons; Screenplay: Barry W. Blaustein & David Sheffield, Tom Shadyac & Steve Oedekerk; Based on the Motion Picture Written By: Jerry Lewis, Bill Richmond; Cinematographer: Julio Macat; Editor: Don Zimmerman; Music: David Newman; Cast: Dave Chappelle, James Coburn, Larry Miller, Jamal Mixon, Eddie Murphy, Jada Pinkett Smith, Doug Williams, Patricia Wilson.

Inside Sherman Klump, a party animal is about to break out.

THE MAKING OF THE NUTTY PROFESSOR

- "The way she's clapping saying, 'Oh, my baby!' Instead of saying 'Fabulous!', she says 'Faaabulous!', that's from my grandmother. My grandmother was so happy I was in the movie business, she'd go, 'Ohhhhh, my family's baby's an actor! Eddie, Eddie, Eddie, Eddie!'" (Vault n.d.) – Eddie Murphy (Actor)
- "Eddie Murphy is one of the five funniest men in the world. When he had to do fart jokes, he lost me. As a matter of fact, I told his editor, if he wants any more from me on a creative level, tell him to pull the whole sequence." (Nashawaty 2011) – Jerry Lewis (Executive Producer)
- "Eddie was so humble on that set. I'm not saying he was so humble as the result of his last few movies not doing so well, but he was so humble for that opportunity of doing *The Nutty Professor*. It's almost like that boxer who lost the fight and was eager to get back into the ring." (Up n.d.) – Doug Williams (Actor)
- "Unless you've got a thing against flatulence jokes, this is one of the funniest movies of the 1990s and an otherworldly

achievement for comedic performance." (Woodroof 2024) – *USA Today*

- "[Eddie Murphy] delivers a heartfelt speech ('Buddy's who I thought I wanted to be–who I thought the world wanted me to be. But I was wrong'). Eddie Murphy looks straight at the camera as he hits the last line, and it occurred to me that maybe he was referring indirectly to some of his recent career miscues." (Ebert 1996) – *The Chicago Sun-Times*

On the domestic box office opening weekend of June 28-30, 1996, *The Nutty Professor* opened in 1st place (Mojo, Domestic 1996 Weekend 26 n.d.). In 4th place was the other major new release of the weekend, *Striptease* (1996) starring Demi Moore and Burt Reynolds.

REVIEW

Remakes can be a bit dodgy. They are either watered down remakes of the original (if that's the case, why bother?) or mostly new films that take light inspiration from the original. Eddie Murphy's remake of Jerry Lewis' *The Nutty Professor* takes the central premise of the original but executes it in its own way, giving a fun spin on a comedy classic.

Sick and tired of his obesity, sugary sweet Professor Sherman Klump (Eddie Murphy) develops a formula to shed those pounds. Unfortunately, this has the side effect of turning him into Buddy Love (Eddie Murphy), a nasty alter-ego who's willing to do anything to get what he wants. As Klump and Love fight for the love of Carla Purty (Jada Pinkett Smith), the former develops a serum to get rid of his thinner, badder side once and for all.

The main attraction here is Eddie Murphy going hog wild on playing a total of seven (!!!) characters in the film. Not only does Murphy play the lead dual role of Sherman Klump (a character so sympathetic you can't help but love him) and Buddy Love (Murphy at the most acerbic he's been since *Eddie Murphy: Raw*), but he also plays four members of the Klump family along with a brief appearance as Lance Perkins (a very funny Richard Simmons parody). A dinner scene full of Klumps and farts is both satirical and riotous. Murphy's work as the mother Anna Pearl Jensen-Klump is especially funny with her egging on her nephew Ernie (Jamal Mixon) calling him "Hercules! Hercules!"; despite this gag being milked, it never wears out its welcome.

Any time the film goes to the romantic comedy exploits between Klump and Purty, the film doesn't work as well. Jada Pinkett Smith (*A Low Down Dirty Shame* (1994), *Woo* (1998)) often holds her own, but the audience is really here to see Murphy's wacky antics. Any inherent drama in whether Klump gets the girl or not is secondary to the slapstick sequences of him trying to play it cool as his formula wears off. Despite some pacing issues, director Tom Shadyac (*Ace Ventura: Pet Detective* (1994), *Patch Adams* (1998)) manages to move scenes along well enough, often favoring wide shots for comedic effect.

Larry Miller (*Radioland Murders* (1994), *What's the Worst That Could Happen?* (2001) is really good here as the conniving Dean Richmond. A classic sort of foil in the vein of John Vernon's turn as Dean Wormer in *Animal House* (1978), Miller's pointed insults at Klump make Murphy's character all the more sympathetic.

A rather decent take on a comedy classic, *The Nutty Professor* lets Eddie Murphy loose in a variety of ways thanks to him playing loads of different characters. He does both great comedic and dramatic work here. A remake of a Jerry Lewis movie shouldn't be this good.

Nutty Professor II: The Klumps (2000)

(2000, Universal Pictures) Director: Peter Segal; Producers: Jeffrey Katzenberg, Aron Warner, John H. Williams; Screenplay: Barry W. Blaustein & David Sheffield, Paul Weitz & Chris Weitz; Story: Steve Oedekerk, Barry W. Blaustein & David Sheffield; Based on Characters Created By: Jerry Lewis, Bill Richmond; Cinematographer: Dean Semler; Editor: William Kerr; Music: David Newman; Cast: Earl Boen, Chris Elliott, Richard Grant, Janet Jackson, Larry Miller, Jamal Mixon, Eddie Murphy, Wanda Sykes.

Eddie Murphy is The Klumps.

THE MAKING OF NUTTY PROFESSOR II: THE KLUMPS

- ""I like to do character stuff and do makeup. I always wonder how come other actors don't do it because it kind of frees you up in terms of what you can do onscreen." (itzjakebitch n.d.) – Eddie Murphy (Actor)
- "I think he's in his best mood when he's playing Poppa; he's at his most playful. Granny, he's the funniest. Sherman, he's the most delightful. Momma is just a person unto herself; there's no Eddie in there." (H. F. Archive 2024) – Peter Segal (Director)
- "They did a lot with blue screens. I'd have to act in scenes with Eddie, and he wouldn't even be on the set. I'd be saying my lines to this tennis ball sitting on a metal stand. Or to a big X on a black flag. It got pretty weird sometimes." (Staff, NUTTY PROFESSOR II: THE KLUMPS 2000) – Janet Jackson (Actress)
- "When a dog's DNA gets mixed in with Buddy's (don't ask), I laughed out loud at a couple of Murphy's sudden transformations into compulsive canine behavior. More

often, sad to say, it's the movie that's the dog." (Ansen 2000)
– *Newsweek*

- "Murphy's characters here seem to personify both his best and worst images of himself, as well as the ways in which blacks traditionally have been caricatured in Hollywood. He needs a movie to match the artist he has become." (Ranier 2000) – *New York Magazine*

On its opening box office weekend of July 28-30, 2000, *Nutty Professor II: The Klumps* crushed the competition with an opening in 1st place (Mojo, Domestic 2000 Weekend 30 n.d.). The other major new release that weekend was the live-action theatrical film *Thomas and the Magic Railroad* (2000) starring Alec Baldwin, which had a far weaker opening in 9th place.

REVIEW

One of the most celebrated scenes in Eddie Murphy's remake of *The Nutty Professor* was the dinner scene where we got to see him play nearly all the parts of the titular character's family, the Klumps. Naturally, when it was time to do the sequels, the family members got a bigger role. *Nutty Professor II: The Klumps* may not be a better film than *The Nutty Professor*, but at times it's a funnier one.

Striving to get rid of his callous alter-ego Buddy Love (Eddie Murphy) once and for all, Professor Sherman Klump (Eddie Murphy) manages to screw up his cure, causing Buddy Love to become an actual separate person. His new girlfriend Denise (Janet Jackson) tries to make sense of the madness as Buddy, Sherman, and the Klumps chase after a de-aging formula that will prove disastrous in the wrong hands.

It has a bit of a labored start, but once it gets going, this film really strives for the madcap lunacy of a classic Bugs Bunny cartoon. Whether it's Dean Richmond (Larry Miller) being sodomized by a hamster or the Klumps getting horny as hell thanks to the youth formula, much of the film feels like a real live wire.

One strength of *Nutty Professor II: The Klumps* is that it lets Eddie Murphy let loose a bit more; the humor doesn't feel as tampered down and reminds one of the edgier material present earlier in Eddie's career. His work as Ida Mae, the Granny of the Klumps, is especially funny here as she tends to be the most outrageous.

Janet Jackson is not that great as the new love interest for the film. She's good at being sincere but doesn't feel as lively as Jada Pinkett did in the last movie. It's also a big pill to swallow seeing Janet Jackson play a DNA researcher; this is about as incongruous as Denise Richards playing a nuclear physicist in the mediocre James Bond film *The World Is Not Enough* (1999).

More amusing than one might assume, *Nutty Professor II: The Klumps* is a solid sequel that can lean a bit too hard on the madcap energy at times, but at least it feels like it's going for broke. Raunchy enough to feel like it should have been R-rated at times (an Uncensored Director's Cut came out later on DVD), *Nutty Professor II: The Klumps* is a solid effort.

Shrek (2001)

(2001, DreamWorks Pictures) Directors: Andrew Adamson, Vicky Jenson; Producers: Jeffrey Katzenberg, Aron Warner, John H. Williams; Screenplay: Ted Elliott & Terry Rossio and Joe Stillman & Roger S.H. Schulman; Additional Dialogue: Cody Cameron & Chris Miller, Conrad Vernon; Based on the Book By: William Steig; Editor: Sim Evan-Jones; Music: Harry Gregson-Williams, John Powell; Cast: Cody Cameron, Vincent Cassel, Jim Cummings, Cameron Diaz, Kathleen Freeman, John Lithgow, Eddie Murphy, Mike Myers.

The greatest fairy tale never told.

THE MAKING OF SHREK

- "To be able to take this new, cutting-edge technology and be able to get good actors, get them together, tell a great story, and to get that all together and it works and it's funny too? It's timeless, you know?" (Insider n.d.) – Eddie Murphy (Actor)
- "To me, the greatest performance Eddie Murphy has ever given is actually in *Shrek*. Donkey is so pure Eddie Murphy. It's 110-proof Eddie Murphy." (All-Access n.d.) – Jeffrey Katzenberg (Producer)
- "One of the really fun things when you're working on an animated film is the process of characterization design, or what you could call character psyche design. It was really fascinating on *Shrek*, because all four main characters are organized around the concept of self-esteem, and appropriate and/or inappropriate reactions to appropriate or inappropriate self-assessment." (Steve and Shewman 2016) – Terry Rossio (Screenwriter)

- "That's one very, very beautiful thing about this movie. As outrageous, and funny and adult as it is in so many ways, at heart it says to kids exactly what they need to hear, which is be happy with who you are." (WFAA n.d.) – John Lithgow (Actor)
- "You'd have to be a bit of an ogre yourself to object to this storybook romance, and the twist in the tale is a nice reproof to the Sleeping Beauty-Snow White legends of transformation." (Quinn 2001) – *The Independent*
- "What I don't want is to gaze at Princess Fiona, at the multifarious play of her near-human features, and wonder if she is supposed to resemble Cameron Diaz." (Lane 2001) – *The New Yorker*

In its opening domestic box office weekend of May 18-20, 2001, *Shrek* opened in 1st place (Mojo, Domestic 2001 Weekend 20 n.d.). The other major new release that weekend was the Jennifer Lopez thriller *Angel Eyes* (2001) which opened in fourth place.

REVIEW

Released six years after Pixar kicked off the CG-animated feature boom with *Toy Story* (1995) and very loosely based off a book by William Steig, *Shrek* manages to be a fairytale spoof that entertains both children (fart jokes, Disneyland references) and adults (a Gingerbread Man getting tortured, phallic Pinocchio gags). A smash hit by anyone's standards (while Dreamworks Animation had done animated features before *Shrek*, this was their first colossal success), *Shrek* is at times a more modest film than some might expect that launched a flurry of sequels, a Broadway musical, and theme park attractions.

Shrek (Mike Myers) is a scary ogre that lives in a swamp who lacks social graces and any sort of companionship. After Lord Farquaad (John Lithgow) relocates unwanted creatures to his abode, Shrek decides to confront him to get his swamp back to the way it was before. On his quest, Shrek meets Donkey (Eddie Murphy) and competes in a contest to rescue Princess Fiona (Cameron Diaz), but Lord Farquaad has other things in mind.

Packed with a soundtrack that jolts viewers between a rousing adventure score by Harry Gregson-Williams and John Powell and hits from the radio ("All Star", "Hallelujah"), *Shrek* lets viewers know this is no ordinary fairytale. The humor comes on fast and furious to varied effects.

A big part of what anchors the film is Mike Myers' (*54* (1998), *Austin Powers: The Spy Who Shagged Me* (2002)) grounded performance of Shrek with a Scottish brogue. Shrek is both a scary and lonely character, and his growth from a grumpy ogre into a more heroic one gives the story a lot of heart.

Eddie Murphy as Donkey is very funny, and his expert line delivery can make lines funny even when there's not much to go on. Who would have thought "And in the morning, I'm making waffles!" would be one of the funniest lines in the film? John Lithgow

(*Footloose* (1984), *Cliffhanger* (1993)) has his moments as the arch Lord Farquaad, although he's not exactly scary enough to be the most compelling villain.

While the beginning swamp material can feel a bit labored, *Shrek* really picks up when the characters arrive to Duloc which parodies theme parks with a Ye Olde Souvenir Shop, a "Welcome to Duloc" opening number not unlike "It's a Small World" from Disneyland, and long queues. Although the plot is often episodic up until this point, the conceit of a contest to win Fiona gives the story more focus once Shrek and Donkey arrive in Duloc.

The big twist at the end of the film with Fiona's character is surprisingly moving, giving the story the extra emotional punch it so badly needs proving that there's more to this story than just loads of jokes. Without the ending and its message of acceptance, *Shrek* wouldn't be the classic it is today.

Shrek 2 (2004)

(2004, DreamWorks Pictures) Directors: Andrew Adamson, Kelly Asbury, Conrad Vernon; Producers: David Lipman, Aron Warner, John H. Williams; Screenplay: Andrew Adamson, Joe Stillman, J. David Stern & David N. Weiss; Story: Andrew Adamson; Based on the Book By: William Steig; Editors: Michael Andrews, Sim-Evan Jones; Music: Harry Gregson-Williams; Cast: Julie Andrews, Antonio Banderas, Cameron Diaz, Rupert Everett, Larry King, Eddie Murphy, Jennifer Saunders, Mike Myers.

The daring hero is back!

THE MAKING OF SHREK 2

- "Some actors need to use their body to be able to communicate with the audience. Some actors can do it with their voices. That's why [*Shrek 2*] is special… They use actors whose voices jump out at you!" (Kinowetter n.d.) – Eddie Murphy (Actor)
- "They had Jennifer Saunders sing the vocals [for "Holding Out for a Hero"], but used the backing tracks from the original song – which might have sounded good 20 years ago, but it sounded really cheesy and was totally unusable, really! The idea was to soup up the production behind the song with drums and bass… And then to try to score the film at that same point – it was a real challenge." (Goldwasser 2004) – Harry Gregson-Williams (Composer)
- "[The screenplay] was wonderfully funny, very, very touching, and, above all, funnily enough, so intelligent, so smart. I loved it! So, when they said, 'Will you be in it?', I said, 'Well, this is the one.'" (T. J. Archive n.d.) – John Cleese (Actor)

- "Much of the story finds Shrek, Princess Fiona and Donkey in a Land Of Far Far Away that's a live ringer for present-day Hollywood, complete with Bowl, Oscar ceremonies, a sun-struck, palm-lined thoroughfare called Romeo Drive and Pinocchio doing Tom Cruise in *Mission Impossible.* Yet there's an old-Hollywood feel to the movie's solid showmanship and unabashed sophistication." (Morgenstern 2004) – *The Wall Street Journal*
- "Shrek 2 discharges its first fart joke — newlyweds Shrek (Mike Myers) and Fiona (Cameron Diaz) making bubbles in a mud bath during their honeymoon — before the opening credits roll, beating the original." (Keough 2004) – *The Boston Phoenix*

On its opening domestic box office weekend of May 21-23, 2004, *Shrek 2* opened in 1st place as the only new major release of the weekend. It beat out films in a variety of genres including *Troy* (2004), *Van Helsing* (2004), and *Mean Girls* (2004).

REVIEW

If the original *Shrek* focused a lot on the titular ogre's stinky swamp existence, *Shrek 2* takes viewers more into the high society royal trappings of Princess Fiona as Shrek gets to meet his wife's parents. *Shrek 2* is packed with so many characters and events it can feel a bit exhausting, but the enthusiasm of the animation and acting help carry things through.

After meeting Princess Fiona's parents King Harold (John Cleese) and Queen Lillian (Julie Andrews), Shrek (Mike Myers) is ashamed of his bad behavior making a bad impression on his wife's parents. As King Harold arranges for Shrek's untimely death so his daughter can marry Prince Charming (Rupert Everett), Shrek tries to patch things up the only clumsy way he can.

Antonio Banderas (*Ballistic: Ecks vs. Sever* (2002), *The Legend of Zorro* (2005)) is just astounding here as the cute yet deadly Puss in Boots giving several sly line readings. Another solid addition is Jennifer Saunders (*Absolutely Fabulous: The Movie* (2016), *Patrick the Pug* (2018)) as the Fairy Godmother who sings a cover of "Holding Out For a Hero" while an intense action scene goes on. Recall in the original *Footloose* film, "Holding Out For a Hero" plays during a tractor game of chicken between Kevin Bacon and Jim Youngs. The epic number somehow feels more at home in *Shrek 2* given its fantasy trappings.

The increased focus on action and spectacle makes *Shrek 2* feel less character-driven than the original, but it also makes it less of a slog. Directors Andrew Adamson, Kelly Asbury, and Conrad Vernon create a mostly nice balance between its boatload of character moments, film parodies, and story beats.

The fracas between Shrek and Fiona's parents is a nice beat in the beginning of the film. It would have been nice to see Shrek and his in-laws getting into a few more arguments of verbal sparring before the plot lurches into its standard sort of hero's journey where

Shrek overcomes obstacles to get a magic thing that won't solve all of the problems he hopes it will.

Eddie Murphy and Antonio Banderas play off well together as Donkey and Puss in Boots. Donkey's dunderhead persona is a nice counterpoint to Puss' wily ways; the former is naive while the latter is world-weary. Puss has gotten two spin-off films to date with Donkey set to get his own feature.

John Cleese (*Fierce Creatures* (1997), *The Pink Panther 2* (2009)) gets a meaty part with King Harold; there's a lot more to it than the usual "aren't rich people stuffy" comedy inherent in such roles. Julie Andrews (*Mary Poppins* (1964), *S.O.B.* (1981)) as Queen Lillian gets a bit less to do as far as the plot goes, but her regal attitude sells the part in a big way.

Shrek 2 is both a lot of fun and a rare animated sequel that's actually worth a watch. It might lack the heart of the first, but it's a lot more fun.

Shrek the Third (2007)

(2007, DreamWorks Animation, Paramount Pictures) Director: Chris Miller, Raman Hui; Producer: Aron Warner; Screenplay: Jeffrey Price & Peter S. Seaman, Chris Miller & Aron Warner; Story: Andrew Adamson; Editor: Michael Andrews, Joyce Arrastia; Based on the Book By: William Steig; Music: Harry Gregson-Williams; Cast: Antonio Banderas, Cameron Diaz, Eric Idle, John Krasinski, Eddie Murphy, Mike Myers, Cheri Oteri, Justin Timberlake.

He's in for the royal treatment.

THE MAKING OF SHREK THE THIRD

- "The original hook concept was 'Shrek reinvents the Arthurian legend.' [...] After a while, you realize, 'Oh, the problem here is, we're not telling a Shrek movie. We're telling an Arthur story, with Shrek supporting it.' It was good, but it just wasn't working." (Armstrong 2007) – Chris Miller (Writer/Director)
- "Merlin's a very mystical person in the Grail and all those legends, so to reduce him into a sort of broken down high school teacher of magic is very funny." (Levyznin n.d.) – Eric Idle (Actor)
- "It's so interesting to me that I'm in a scene with Julie Andrews because *The Sound of Music* was such a huge film for me when I was a kid. Those things really stick with you when you're young. Knowing you're going to be part of a thing that these kids are going to remember forever, that's kind of the coolest thing about it." (AllTrailersMov n.d.) – Justin Timberlake (Actor)
- "At a brisk 93 minutes, this merely reheats the franchise's old familiar elements (plenty of poo and bum jokes for the kids

and cine-literate nods for the adults, including *The Exorcist* via *Rosemary's Baby* and *The Brood*) to give us more - or, rather, less - of the same." (Kermode 2007) – *The Guardian*

- "Where the first "Shrek" left me elated, this one never touched my heart or got under my skin." (Ansen, No More Mickey Mouse: Animation for Adults 2007) – *Newsweek*

Shrek the Third smashed the competition in 1st place on its opening domestic box office weekend of May 18-20, 2007 (Mojo, Domestic 2007 Weekend 20 n.d.). Popular movies it beat out for the weekend included *Spider-Man 3* (2007) and *28 Weeks Later* (2007), although *Shrek the Third* was the only major new release in theaters that weekend.

REVIEW

Sequels to animated features are tricky to get right. They are a lot like sequels to comedies where they often feature the same gags in a slightly different scenario and no real arc or compelling motivation for the main characters. *Shrek the Third* takes this tired lazy route that feels like a Shrek movie developed on autopilot with little of the wit or charm of the first two entries.

After King Harold (John Cleese) dies, Shrek (Mike Myers) and Fiona (Cameron Diaz) learn that another heir lies in waiting for the throne, Artie Pendragon (Justin Timberlake). As Shrek goes to find Artie with Donkey (Eddie Murphy) and Puss in Boots (Antonio Banderas), he discovers that his wife Fiona is now pregnant. To complicate the plot even more, Prince Charming (Rupert Everett) and Captain Hook (Ian McShane) plan to assassinate Shrek and Artie.

Shrek the Third suffers from a bloated plot and an awfully weak premise. Shrek and Fiona not becoming the new King and Queen isn't the stuff of high drama. To make matters worse, the character of Artie (a teenage take on King Arthur) is played as such a whiny little shit by Justin Timberlake (*Edison* (2005), *Runner Runner* (2013)) that he's hard to root for. It makes audiences not invested in the big quest for Shrek and his buddies to find Artie and bring him back to the castle.

Just because you can make a sequel doesn't mean you should. Nothing feels really new with this take on Shrek. It feels tired and rather by the numbers. That's not to say *Shrek the Third* is unwatchable. Eric Idle (*Monty Python Live at the Hollywood Bowl* (1982), *Nuns on the Run* (1990)) is fitfully amusing playing a rather beleaguered Merlin the Magician. There's a moment where Puss and Donkey swap bodies where Eddie Murphy and Antonio Banderas get to have a *Face/Off* (1997) sort of moment.

One of the most so-so cartoon sequels in quite some time, *Shrek the Third* waters down the characters and the central premise so much that you begin to forget why you loved the series in the first place. A truly hum-drum affair, *Shrek the Third* is one movie where you are begging for it to be ogre before it's barely started.

Shrek Forever After (2010)

(2010; Paramount Pictures) Director: Mike Mitchell; Producer: Teresa Cheng, Gina Shay; Screenplay: Josh Klausner & Darren Lemke; Based on the Book By: William Steig; Cinematographer: Yong Duk Jhun; Editor: Nick Fletcher; Music: Harry Gregson-Williams; Cast: Julie Andrews, Antonio Banderas, John Cleese, Cameron Diaz, Walt Dohrn, Jon Hamm, Eddie Murphy, Mike Myers.

It ain't ogre... Til it's ogre.

THE MAKING OF SHREK FOREVER AFTER

- "It's a little edgier than the other *Shrek* movies... I think what really holds the movies together is the relationship between Shrek and Fiona, and that you connect emotionally with those two characters." (CELEBS.com n.d.) – Eddie Murphy (Actor)
- "[*Shrek the Third*] was not a good movie. Now everybody hates Shrek. Again, I was the underdog. No one wanted to work on [*Shrek Forever After*]." (Taylor 2024) – Mike Mitchell (Director)
- "I think that Shrek is a little bit like Flintstones vitamins. You don't know that it's good for you, but it has built-in vitamins and the delivery system is very enjoyable." (Weintraub 2010) – Mike Myers (Actor)
- "Having loved the original film nine years ago, then largely missed out on the next two, I was shocked to see the new film driven by such ennui. Is this still for the young, I wondered, as I tried to adjust my 3D glasses to lose the milky film and edge blur that comes with some 3D movies. What kid cares about a midlife crisis?" (Bynes 2010) – *The Sydney Morning Herald*

- "Yes, it helps that this one is in 3-D – the real deal, not a retrofit – that makes the action pop. But it's the characters that pull us in when familiarity flatlines our interest." (Travers, Shrek Forever After 2010) – *Rolling Stone*

On its opening domestic box office weekend, *Shrek Forever After* opened in 1st place, beating out *Iron Man 2* (2010) in its 3rd week. Despite all the Shrek movies making hundreds of millions of dollars, *Shrek Forever After* has been the most recent Shrek movie in the series that's not a spin-off in over a decade. They've done two Puss in Boots theatrical films to date (*Puss in Boots* (2011) and *Puss in Boots: The Last Wish* (2022)) and a gaggle of shorts and made for TV Shrek specials in the meantime. A fifth Shrek movie and a spin-off movie focused on Eddie Murphy's Donkey character is in the works.

REVIEW

It's a rare thing for the fourth film in a series to be one of the best (originally, *Shrek Forever After* was marketed as *Shrek The Final Chapter*), but *Shrek Forever After* takes a thoughtful premise inspired by Frank Capra's *It's a Wonderful Life* (1946) and delivers. Like an onion, a *Shrek* sequel can have layers after all.

After arguing with Fiona (Cameron Diaz), Shrek (Mike Myers) accepts an offer from Rumpelstiltskin (Walt Dohrn) to live a day as a single man again. After being transported to an alternate reality where ogres have formed a resistance army against King Rumpelstiltskin, Shrek is forced to rethink his choices.

A good part of why *Shrek Forever After* works so well is the clever screenplay by Josh Klausner (*Date Night* (2010), *Wanderland* (2018)) & Darren Lemke (*Gemini Man* (2019), *Goosebumps 2: Haunted Halloween*). By committing to an alternate reality concept (think the old Marvel "What If?" comics), it resets the table and gives characters real stakes again.

Although Rumpelstiltskin has been a tried-and-true villain in movies and television for decades, the snarky angle of *Shrek Forever After*'s take on the character really brings it to life. In an unusual move, Rumpelstiltskin is voiced by Walt Dohrn (*Mr. Peabody & Sherman* (2014), *Trolls Band Together* (2023)), one of Dreamworks Animations' long-time story artists and writers. By not sticking to the all-star celebrity voice casting for which *Shrek* is known for, Walt Dohrn provides an unhinged memorable performance for a major character in the film. Although there is precedence for this (Andrew Stanton voiced the stoner surfer turtle Crush and also directed *Finding Nemo* (2003)), it's a casting choice more animated feature films should take note of.

Eddie Murphy and Mike Myers seem a bit more energized this time around as Donkey and Shrek respectively. By reinventing their characters a bit given the movie's clever scenario, their performances positively pop. The angle of ogres forming a resistance group that feels a bit like something out of *Lord of the Rings: The Two Towers* (2002) can get a bit muddled, but, again, the change of scenery helps liven it along. Cameron Diaz gets more to do as Fiona this time around driving the story forward as a real warrior; she's not played just for laughs.

One of the better animated films in not-so-recent memory, *Shrek Forever After* is quite a coup for the series. Whenever the fifth *Shrek* movie comes out, one hopes it will continue this wildly creative streak.

The Hidden Gems

Boomerang (1992)

(1992; Paramount Pictures) Director: Reginald Hudlin; Producer: Brian Grazer, Warrington Hudlin; Screenplay: Barry W. Blaustein & David Sheffield; Story: Eddie Murphy; Cinematographer: Woody Omens; Editor: John Carter, Michael Jablow, Earl Watson; Music: Marcus Miller; Cast: Halle Berry, Tisha Campbell, Robin Givens, David Alan Grier, Grace Jones, Martin Lawrence, Eddie Murphy, John Witherspoon.

Player Who's About to be Played.

THE MAKING OF BOOMERANG

- "The most political thing about *Boomerang* is that it's a movie with an all-black cast, and it has nothing to do with being black or nothing. They're just people." (Biz n.d.) – Eddie Murphy (Actor/Writer)
- "*Boomerang* really captured who we were at the time. Back then, we were both young single guys living in New York going to the clubs, so we could totally relate to those characters." (Original Cin 2023) – Reginald Hudlin (Director)
- "You have to have total respect for the guy. On the other hand, the process (of filmmaking) can be hard with him. Eddie will approve a scene on a Tuesday, then you get to Thursday and he'll rethink it. And you've already spent a lot of money. But to his credit, he's usually right about everything." (Berkman 1992) – Brian Grazer (Producer)
- "What goes around, comes around is the movie's message. The problem with such thinking is that it traps us in an endless boomerang cycle in which instead of progressing,

we just keep repeating the same screwed-up patterns of the past." (Baumgarten 1992) – *The Austin Chronicle*

- "This 1992 Eddie Murphy comedy starts out like a warmed-over Frank Sinatra vehicle of the 50s or 60s, but before long it becomes clear that Murphy—who's credited with the story that Barry W. Blaustein and David Sheffield's script is based on—is interested in critiquing, perhaps even dismantling, the narcissistic womanizer he's been playing for years." (Rosenbaum, Boomerang n.d.) – *The Chicago Reader*

On its opening weekend on the 4th of July weekend in 1992, *Boomerang* opened in 3rd place at the domestic box office. Above it in 1st and 2nd place, respectively, were *Batman Returns* (1992) and *A League of Their Own* (1992).

REVIEW

Eddie Murphy was clearly trying something different and more adult for his career with *Boomerang*. Yes, there's the regular raunchiness audiences have come to expect, but there's also a slick romantic comedy here in which Murphy gets comeuppance for his womanizing ways. It's a romance that makes you think afterwards and breaks from the usual cute formula, keeping viewers mostly guessing until the end.

Marcus Graham (Eddie Murphy), a hotshot ad executive whose company is in the middle of a merger, is high on his own supply of braggadocio. When he's not seeing his friends Gerard (David Alan Grier) and Tyler (Martin Lawrence), Murphy tries to woo Jacqueline (Robin Givens) and Angela (Halle Berry).

Being a spoof of advertising in the increasingly sex-positive cosmetic industry while also working a credible romantic comedy is a really tough act, but *Boomerang* manages to pull it off. Reginald Hudlin's direction smartly gives the cast time to shine so it's not just Eddie Murphy in the spotlight all the time. Grace Jones (*Vamp* (1986), *Wolf Girl* (2001)) is very funny as the oddball fashion icon Helen Strangé, and David Alan Grier (*Amazon Women on the Moon* (1987), *Little Man* (2006)) has nice moments as the rather nerdy Gerard.

It's a testament to the casting here that there's a mixture of the old guard and the new. Eartha Kitt (*Ernest Scared Stupid* (1991), *Harriet the Spy* (1996)) smolders as the conniving Lady Eloise while Bebe Drake (*Friday After Next* (2002), *Jason's Lyric* (1994)) and John Witherspoon (*Killer Tomatoes Strike Back!* (1991), *I'm Gonna Git You Sucka* (1988)) make for hilarious parents bickering over every little thing they come across.

Above all else, *Boomerang* really makes one feel for Marcus' plight. Despite his flashy car and flashier duds, Marcus is a man lost at sea. His love life has been a series of one-night stands, but he's looking for something deeper. As he learns in the film, sometimes you don't know what you've got until it's gone.

Marcus is an especially great role at this point in Eddie Murphy's career because his character is doing more than cracking hilarious jokes the entire time or being the smartest man in the room. More than being a live-action Bugs Bunny in the "ain't I a stinker?" mode, he's playing a real person with real problems. Eddie's commitment to the part really sells the emotional stakes at hand.

One of the stronger entries in Eddie Murphy's comedic career as a whole, *Boomerang* does what all romantic comedies aspire to: it works both as a romance and a comedy in equal measure. This is one *Boomerang* you won't mind coming back to.

Bowfinger (1999)

(1999; Universal Pictures) Director: Frank Oz; Producer: Brian Grazer; Screenplay: Steve Martin; Cinematographer: Ueli Steiger; Editor: Richard Pearson; Music: David Newman; Cast: Christine Baranski, John Cho, Robert Downey Jr., Heather Graham, Jamie Kennedy, Steve Martin, Eddie Murphy, Terence Stamp.

The Con is On.

THE MAKING OF BOWFINGER

- "I like the subversive quality in movies. There has to be that edge. And when you make edginess acceptable to the audience, it becomes funny." (Breznican n.d.) – Frank Oz (Director)
- "You know, I wanted a movie that would play well in Europe. Very physical comedy. And the biggest challenge in physical comedy, most importantly, is not to become too stupid, but for it to be clever, because otherwise you're just falling down. I was talking to Frank Oz about this. He said, 'We can't just have the ladder whack somebody. We've got to have the ladder whack somebody because of X, Y and Z having been set up, and it's inevitable the ladder is whacking us.'" (Fisher 1999) – Steve Martin (Actor/Writer)
- "*Bowfinger* is just amazing. Working with auteurs like Steve [Martin] and Frank [Oz] and Eddie [Murphy]… Steve wrote it and starred in it, and he knew what he wanted. I played his sidekick. And just getting to work with guys like that… It was like being able to go to school, I learned so much from it at the knee of greatness." (W. Harris 2020) – Jamie Kennedy (Actor)

- "The screenplay for *Bowfinger* was written by Martin, and it's not always sharp (the first 10 minutes are especially slow, and there are moments when the humor seems outdated). But Martin can be a brilliant gag writer when he mines the opportunity for absurdity, and *Bowfinger* gets better and better as the story grows less plausible." (Klosterman 1999) – *The Akron Beacon Journal*
- "Martin the writer plants some wicked barbs in Hollywood's rear end about creative financing of movies and hoarding of profits, the art of the deal, hipper-than-thou attitudes and exploitation. When Bowfinger rounds up migrant workers as his crew, some viewers are going to be shocked, but they need to ride it out. Martin gives it a neat spin." (Graham 1999) – *The San Francisco Chronicle*

Bowfinger debuted domestically on August 13-15, 1999, in 2nd place (Box Office Mojo n.d.). Beating it in 1st place was the M. Night Shyamalan classic *The Sixth Sense* (1999). *Bowfinger* did manage to beat out one new major release that also debuted the same weekend, the Claire Dane and Kate Beckinsale thriller *Brokedown Palace* (1999).

REVIEW

Steve Martin (*Grand Canyon* (1991), *The Man with Two Brains* (1983)) and Eddie Murphy were two of the biggest comedians of the 1980s and 1990s. To see them both in a film together seemed like the comedic equivalent of the 1992 United States Men's Olympic Basketball Dream Team featuring such legends as Michael Jordan, Scottie Pippen, Magic Johnson, and Charles Barkley. Steve Martin's script provides a smart, satirical take on Hollywood that makes one wish he would team up with Eddie Murphy again.

Cheapskate producer Bobby Bowfinger (Steve Martin) schemes to film a movie starring star Kit Ramsey (Eddie Murphy) by shooting him in secret. To complete his footage, he works with Jiff Ramsey (Eddie Murphy), a nerdy dead ringer for Kit.

Poking fun at everything from Scientology to naive actresses, *Bowfinger* is a hoot and a half. Steve Martin plays the flim-flam producer with a nice blend of cheapness and anger that we've seen in roles he's played before.

Eddie Murphy is asked to do a lot more of the heavy-lifting playing either a bratty movie star (Eddie Murphy on his worst days on set?) or a naive lookalike whose long pauses and breathing come off as slightly creepy (the worst Eddie Murphy fan encounter writ large?). Murphy is never afraid here to play characters who look bad or foolish; everything is done in service of the comedy, and the movie is better for it. Part of why Murphy is so good here is the contrasts between how the characters talk; Kit speaks a mile a minute while Jiff is slower and deliberate, albeit being a much nicer person. Both characters are anxious for completely different reasons.

Terence Stamp provides a nice spacey pomposity as Terry Stricter, Kit's guru at Mind Head, an organization not unlike Scientology. Heather Graham (*License to Drive* (1988), *Killing Me Softly* (2002)) is quite effective as a ditzy actress who's new in town insisting she'd do "anything" for a part; the anything being in emphatic capital letters to make sure nobody misses her unsubtle points.

It's lovely how *Bowfinger*'s team-up of Steve Martin and Eddie Murphy doesn't aim for the lowest common denominator. Those who don't care how a movie is made might be a bit bored at times by the sluggish first act, but once things get going, this is a fun ride indeed unusually full of suspense for a comedy. Will *Bowfinger* and his crew get caught following Kit around or get away with it again?

Interview with Jade Greenberg

(USA Today Best-Selling Author)

Which of Eddie Murphy's skits from *SNL* stand out to you??

"Mr. Robinson's Neighborhood" is one of the best *SNL* skits of all time. "White Like Me" was genius. Those two are the most prevalent in my memory.

How did Eddie's persona change over the years when he made the transition from comedy to family films?

When you have kids, I imagine you want to make content they can consume. I'm not sure what his motivations were, but that would be my guess - he became a father, and his persona either intentionally or coincidentally accommodated that.

Whether that shift was intentional, I don't know, but films like *Daddy Day Care* are very much aligned with a more mature and paternal persona.

You've mentioned *Bowfinger* is one of your favorite Eddie Murphy movies. Why that one in particular?

Eddie Murphy gave one of the best comedic performances in film history in *Bowfinger*, and Eddie Murphy alongside Steve Martin is one of my favorite comedic combinations. *Bowfinger* is the ultimate example!

Do you think Eddie would be good in a Broadway show? He was rumored to make a return to stand-up comedy until the COVID-19 pandemic changed those plans.

Eddie has everything a performer needs to deliver a brilliant performance on a Broadway stage, but if I had to choose between him doing a Broadway show or doing another stand-up special, I'd choose stand-up. I'd love to hear what he has to say about the world today!

Candy Cane Lane (2003)

(2023; Amazon Studios) Director: Reginald Hudlin; Producer: Brian Grazer, Charisse M. Hewitt, Karen Lunder, Eddie Murphy; Screenplay: Kelly Younger; Cinematographer: Eric Steelberg; Editor: Kenny G. Krauss, Jim May; Music: Marcus Miller; Cast: Jillian Bell, David Alan Grier, Ken Marino, Eddie Murphy, Nick Offerman, Chris Redd, Timothy Simons, Tracee Ellis Ross.

You Can't Escape the Holiday Magic.

THE MAKING OF CANDY CANE LANE

- "We wanted to do something that would be around forever, that people could watch over and over again like the Christmas movies when I was a kid." (America n.d.) – Eddie Murphy (Actor)
- "We had this light system so the real-life action actors would know where to look where the little people would be. We got to shoot it all at once and we got to improvise and then really have fun together." (Ruby 2023) – Reginald Hudlin (Director)
- "There were moments when I came up to Reggie and say, 'I have a big idea', and he'd go, 'OK, there's only one problem… It can be bigger!" (Hass 2023) – Kelly Younger (Screenwriter)
- "For folks who feel holiday movies are too pat and predictable, this one is nutty as a fruitcake. And as with fruitcake, this is a flick some people will love and some people will hate." (Gillmore 2023) – *The Winnipeg Free Press*
- "I wouldn't call "Candy Cane Lane" one of Murphy's good comedies; it's too long, too jammed together, and beneath it all too Christmas cookie cutter. Yet Murphy inhabits the

role of a doting dad who lives for Christmas with reassuring ease." (Gleiberman 2023) – *Variety*

Apart from a handful of screenings, *Candy Cane Lane* made its debut on Prime Video. The first three days of its release on Prime Video, it was the number 1 film globally (Campione 2023). Given its wide appeal and its Christmas setting, *Candy Cane Lane* is a movie that feels like it should have been in theaters.

REVIEW

Christmas movies are one of those tried-and-true genres whether it's *Four Christmases* (2008) or *National Lampoon's Christmas Vacation* (1989). *Candy Cane Lane* goes for a more fantastical vibe than one might expect from its rather generic posters, but it does so with good humor. There are special effects all over the place, but they're in service of the story, which is what matters in the end.

Every year, Chris Carver (Eddie Murphy) competes against his neighbor Bruce (Ken Marino) for which house will have the best Christmas decorations outside the front of their house. After discovering an odd shop called Kringle's, he buys an amazing decoration based on "The Twelve Days of Christmas" song in exchange for paying a terrible price. Before too long, the humans and animals from the song wreak havoc upon the neighborhood and Chris has to save the day or be turned into a living figurine forever.

After an opening that feels like something out of a generic Tim Allen movie, *Candy Cane Lane* finds its footing when it leans into the fantastical elements. ILM's special effects work on the talking figurines which not only reflect light just like a real ornament but also move in the style of the beloved characters from the Rankin-Bass stop-motion TV specials of the 1960s and 1970s, which comes off as quite charming. The extra work put into the special effects keeps the story from feeling cheesy.

Eddie Murphy is playing a role here he's done a lot before where he's a workaholic father who learns the lesson of being more of a family man, but he adds some pathos to his performance when he realizes he might be stuck as a figurine forever as a result of him being in a rush to get the perfect lawn decoration. David Alan Grier is very funny as Santa Claus popping up in the third act of the film.

Jillian Bell (*Good Burger 2* (2023), *Murder Mystery 2* (2023)) plays the scheming elf Pepper with real zeal, making for quite the dastardly foe for Eddie Murphy to play up against. Tracee Ellis Ross

(*American Fiction* (2023), *In the Weeds* (2000)) does nice work as his beleaguered wife Carol who has to try and keep the peace around her as things get nuttier and nuttier as the magical menagerie continues to cut loose.

Candy Cane Lane takes what could have been a boring premise and livens it up with great special effects and a madcap sensibility one might expect from Tim Burton or Terry Gilliam. As long as you can make it through the first few scenes, you'll find there's plenty worth sticking around for in this visit to *Candy Cane Lane*.

The Distinguished Gentleman (1992)

(1992; Buena Vista Pictures) Director: Jonathan Lynn; Producer: Marty Kaplan, Leonard Goldberg, Michael Peyser; Screenplay: Marty Kaplan; Story: Marty Kaplan, Jonathan Reynolds; Cinematographer: Gabriel Beristain; Editor: Barry B. Leirer, Tony Lombardo; Music: Randy Edelman; Cast: Joe Don Baker, Charles S. Dutton, Chi McBride, Kevin McCarthy, Eddie Murphy, Sheryl Lee Ralph, Victoria Rowell, Lane Smith.

From con man to congressman.

THE MAKING OF THE DISTINGUISHED GENTLEMAN

- "How could I be trapped in anything at 31? There are no walls around me. I do what I want to do when I feel like doing it. I never aspired to change, to be like, The New Eddie. I was just being who I am as an artist." (Berkman, Eddie Murphy's second coming 1992) – Eddie Murphy (Actor)
- "If only he'd had Eddie Murphy to show him the ropes, George Santos' grift could have been perfectly legal, and the House Republican conference might still be calling the con man from Queens and Long Island 'the distinguished gentleman from New York.'" (Prigge 2023) – Marty Kaplan (Screenwriter)
- "Wonderful director. He was a terrific director to work with, we had a wonderful relationship. We had a terrific time on *My Cousin Vinny*. Of course, *The Distinguished Gentleman* was one of these great big, massive budget deals, and everybody gets a little uptight on those things." (Simpsons 2015) – Lane Smith (Actor)

Opening domestically in 4th place on December 4-6, 1992, *The Distinguished Gentleman* had the misfortune of going against such whoppers as *Aladdin* (1992), *Home Alone 2: Lost in New York* (1992), and *The Bodyguard* (1992) (Box Office Mojo n.d.). In retrospect, a post-Thanksgiving release doesn't make the most sense for a political satire.

REVIEW

Political satires can be a tricky thing. If they are too comedic, they weaken the believability of the story. If they are too political, they leave audiences wondering where the jokes are. *The Distinguished Gentleman*, with a snappy screenplay by Marty Kaplan and Jonathan Reynolds, manages to stick the landing, making it a bit of a buried treasure in Eddie Murphy's filmography.

Inspired by the corruption Kaplan witnessed during his days as a speech writer in Washington, D.C., *The Distinguished Gentleman* weaves a prescient political fable about Thomas Jefferson Johnson (Eddie Murphy), a con man that happens to have the same middle and last names as Jeff Johnson (James Garner), a Congressman who recently died. It's election season, and Johnson is going to have a go at it.

Eddie Murphy's character has an actual character arc here, going from a slick grifter wetting his beak at every opportune moment to a staunch defender of environmental rights. In the middle of all this is a romance Thomas Jefferson Johnson has with Loretta Hicks (Sheryl Lee Ralph) which really works because she's no mere eye candy; Hicks is integral to the story as a big reason for convincing Johnson to change his ways.

The Distinguished Gentleman does a great job of setting up what a sleazebag Eddie Murphy's character is in the opening sequence at a dinner party full of political elites. He puts on an accent, tries to act like a person of authority when he's not (Murphy nails any scene where he's the guy who walks in like he owns the place), and escapes with his entourage by the skin of his teeth.

The rest of the film could use that opening's snappy pacing. There's a lot of necessary exposition about how politics and funding works in order to set up the later inevitable betrayals, but it's directed by Jonathan Lynn (*Clue* (1985), *Nuns on the Run* (1990)) in a kind of flat manner lacking the punch one would expect. Too often, *The Distinguished Gentleman* has the feel of a lesser 1970s sitcom.

Lane Smith (*The Bad News Bears in Breaking Training* (1977), *Son in Law* (1993)) is especially strong as the dastardly smooth Dick Dodge. Smith's killer cobra smile stresses a core theme in the film: everyone in politics is nice to your face but stabs you in the back in the end. Equally effective is a young Chi McBride (*Cradle 2 The Grave* (2003), *The Frighteners* (1996)) as Homer who shows some strong comedic chops in a small part.

After a sort of saggy middle, *The Distinguished Gentleman* picks up again when Johnson orchestrates a final con to expose Dodge's hypocrisy in front of his political colleagues. In many ways, *The Distinguished Gentleman* allows Murphy to do more dramatic work than he has in the past which enriches every angle of his character. His character is willing to risk his political career for what he believes in, and his transformation is believable; most movies can't pull this off.

A super strong entry in Eddie Murphy's career, *The Distinguished Gentleman* shows off sides of him the audience hasn't seen before with a more realized character that's doing more than cracking wise. Unavailable on streaming services in the United States, it's worth tracking down the non-anamorphic widescreen DVD to add this to your home video library.

Dolemite Is My Name (2019)

(2019; Netflix) Director: Craig Brewer; Producer: Laurence Mark; Screenplay: Scott Alexander, Larry Karaszewski; Cinematographer: Eric Steelberg; Editor: Billy Fox; Music: Scott Bomar; Cast: Titus Burgess, Snoop Dogg, Mike Epps, Keegan-Michael Key, Luenell, Eddie Murphy, Da'Vine Joy Randolph, Wesley Snipes.

Make your own legend.

THE MAKING OF DOLEMITE IS MY NAME

- "I've had this conversation with comedians all the time. They're laughing at [Rudy Ray Moore], saying: 'Look how bad he is. He doesn't realize how bad this is.' I'm like, 'No, no, he knows this is funny.'" (The Independent 2019) – Eddie Murphy (Actor)
- "That was our idea behind the screenplay, but it's been this larger takeaway, which is people saying that the movie inspires them to go create anything they've ever thought about creating, but never got around to doing. That's been really magical." (Phillips 2019) – Scott Alexander (Screenwriter)
- "The cuts and the timing are not quite comedy cuts and timing, but they're not quite drama either." (Tangcay 2020) – Billy Fox (Editor)
- "Alexander and Karaszewski have done for Murphy what they did for Burton: they've gifted him with the film of his career, a deeply observed and felt characterization of a marginal comedic talent who would not let his vision down, no matter how warped it might have been." (Marks 2019) – *The San Diego Reader*

- "Writers Scott Alexander and Larry Karaszewski have made a career of celebrating the outcasts of American culture (*Ed Wood, The People vs. Larry Flynt*, the Andy Kaufman biopic *Man on the Moon*), and here, once again, they find in Moore that unique brand of dignity found only in the defiantly undignified." (Newcott 2019) – *The Saturday Evening Post*

Dolemite Is My Name had a very limited theatrical run but was released on Netflix streaming on October 25, 2019 (McClintock 2019). Given this was one of Eddie's best reviewed movies in years, it would have been nice for it to get a prestige theatrical release with a heavy push for Oscar nominations, but Netflix in particular seems to enjoy dodging any theatrical releases of merit altogether.

REVIEW

Screenwriters Scott Alexander and Larry Karaszewski have made a cottage industry of writing biopics of misfit entrepreneurs as diverse as Andy Kaufman (*Man on the Moon* (1999)) and Larry Flynt (*The People vs. Larry Flynt* (1996)). *Dolemite Is My Name* pairs their trademark witty approach with the sassy directing chops of Craig Brewer (*Hustle & Flow* (2005), *Black Snake Moan* (2006)) to make a funny film about achieving your dreams no matter how ridiculous they might be.

After finding success with a series of underground comedy records, Rudy Ray Moore (Eddie Murphy) sets his sights on the silver screen to make Dolemite, his dream project combining his love of karate, gangsters, and pimps. However, Moore learns making the movie is only one piece of the puzzle. He has one final challenge to complete his quest: find a distributor to get it in theaters.

Among other things, *Dolemite Is My Name* is Eddie Murphy's first rated-R movie since 1997's *Metro*. It's so refreshing to watch Murphy sparkle in a role that lets him be as wiry and unhinged as he was in his earlier 1980s comedies. He doesn't play Rudy Ray Moore as a cartoon; instead, he makes you relate to him as a real person.

One of the best sequences comes early in the film where we see Rudy developing jokes for his first album. Craig Brewer shoots the montage in a very loose style letting viewers see just how hard it is to whittle a joke down to its bone until it snaps with every syllable. It's great fun to watch Eddie Murphy think his way to the smoothest rhythm and best punchlines in this sequence.

Wesley Snipes is fantastic playing character actor D'Urville Martin in outlandish gut-busting fashion. He's so good, it makes one wish Snipes would have done more comedies in his prime. Da'Vine Joy Randolph (*A Little White Lie* (2023), *The Secrets of Emily Blair* (2016)) is also fiery as Lady Reed, a single mother Rudy Ray Moore meets while on tour who becomes a regular in his films.

If nothing else, *Dolemite Is My Name* is a movie about big risks bringing big rewards. A biopic on a blaxploitation star could easily be by the numbers, but *Dolemite Is My Name* has greater ambitions. It has some deep cut references to Rudy Ray Moore's oeuvre (montages of Moore making *Dolemite* are a sort of greatest hits of sequences from his best-known films) while still remaining accessible to someone that's never listened to his records or seen his movies.

One of the best biopics in decades, *Dolemite Is My Name* is a smart comedy celebrating the hard work it takes to make an independent film, making it a sort of companion piece to Scott Alexander and Larry Karaszewski's *Ed Wood* (1994).

Dreamgirls (2016)

(2006; Dreamworks Pictures, Paramount Pictures) Director: Bill Condon; Producer: Laurence Mark; Screenplay: Bill Condon; Based on the Original Broadway Production Book By: Tom Eyen; Cinematographer: Tobias Schliessler; Editor: Virginia Katz; Music: Tom Eyen, Henry Krieger; Cast: Beyoncé, Jamie Foxx, Danny Glover, Jennifer Hudson, Sharon Leal, John Lithgow, Eddie Murphy, Anika Noni Rose.

All you have to do is dream.

THE MAKING OF DREAMGIRLS

- "To prepare for [*Dreamgirls*], I watched a bunch of videos of James Brown, Little Richard, Otis Redding, Jackie Wilson, Samuel Davis, Sam & Dave, so I could learn how to move. I took tiny little pieces from everybody, so I could keep the work within that time period; I had the character moving the way people moved back then, as opposed to dancing like I would feel now." (Leonelli 2023) – Eddie Murphy (Actor)
- "I always thought [*Dreamgirls*] had an amazing story and that there was a reason to tell it now. The passage of time allows you to put it into historical context, and see how remarkable this cultural change was. It's one that we're still playing out today." (Igel 2007) – *Dreamgirls* (Director/Screenwriter)
- "We were more conservative with the camera at the onset; however, as the drama builds, we became more stylized in its movement. One scene in particular was when Curtis and the other Dreams gang up on Effie. We shot the scene with a Steadicam as the girls fought with Effie from various angles." (D'Alessandro 2007) – Tobias Schliessler (Cinematographer)

- "Unlike the film version of *Chicago* (scripted by this film's director, Bill Condon), *Dreamgirls* doesn't feel synthetic and dead on-screen. It uses theatrical conventions to capture some of the energy of live theater; for example, a clever curtain-call-style credit sequence gives the audience a chance to cheer for the actors one by one as we revisit the highlights of each performance." (Stevens 2006) – *Slate*
- "Just how one of those robberies happens is a laugh-out-loud touch, when Jimmy's supposed breakthrough hit, "Cadillac Car," is forever entombed as Pat Boone-style fluff. But it becomes clear that the same sort of sanitization and sterilization has been applied to this take on *Dreamgirls*. When it was scrubbed clean for a shiny glow, it took the soul right out of the story." (Rogers 2006) – *Midwest Film Journal*

Dreamgirls had a soft opening domestic weekend at the box office on December 15-17, 2006, opening in just 3 theaters making its debut in 19th place (Box Office Mojo n.d.). Other major new releases that weekend included the Will Smith drama *The Pursuit of Happyness* (2006), the high fantasy film *Eragon* (2006), and a live-action remake of *Charlotte's Web* (2006) with a creepy realistic CG rendering of the titular spider.

REVIEW

Heavily inspired by the career of The Supremes and based off the hit Broadway musical, *Dreamgirls* is a strong movie musical that gives Eddie Murphy a supporting role that fits him like a glove. Packed with songs and heartfelt drama, *Dreamgirls* is one of the best musicals made for the silver screen in recent memory that propels viewers through the ups and downs of a Motown career so fast they'll get whiplash.

After getting noticed at a talent show at the Detroit Theater, The Dreamettes run into the highs and lows of super stardom as their lives are forever changed by their success. There are ups and downs. Much drama ensues.

Part of the joy in watching *Dreamgirls* is seeing how different songs are created in the studio. Crafting a true hit single takes a lot of work and doesn't spring out of thin air, and this movie takes that approach to heart. Jennifer Hudson (*Chi-Raq* (2015), *Respect* (2021)) makes such a strong debut as Effie White she nearly blows everyone off the screen. Danny Glover (*The Color Purple* (1985), *Death Race 4: Beyond Anarchy* (2018)) is also great in a less showy part as a former manager of James "Thunder" Early.

Speaking of James "Thunder" Early, the role played by Eddie Murphy, it's a pivotal supporting role in the film. A rather lascivious singer who picks up the Dreamettes as his backup dancers early on in the film, Murphy plays the role like he has something to prove. Whether it's singing a musical number ("Fake Your Way to the Top" describes his life philosophy) or acting his heart out in a dramatic scene, Eddie Murphy really shines here. It's a damn shame Eddie Murphy lost a Best Supporting Oscar to Alan Arkin's (*The In-Laws* (1979), *The Return of Captain Invincible* (1983)) twee work in *Little Miss Sunshine* (2006).

Bill Condon shoots the many live musical numbers on stage with a camera that's as energetic and loose as the actors, capturing the vivacity of watching a live performance. In one sequence, the camera appears to dive down the mouth of a trumpet!

One of the best musicals on the silver screen in recent memory, *Dreamgirls* is a stellar example of the genre with strong acting, catchy musical numbers, and a story that's as rich as any soap opera. One for the record books, *Dreamgirls* is an unforgettable film.

Eddie Murphy: Delirious (1983)

(1983; HBO) Director: Bruce Gowers; Producer: Eddie Murphy, Richard Tienken, Robert D. Wachs; Written by: Eddie Murphy; Editor: Ken Denisoff, David Farr; Cast: Eddie Murphy.

Strictly for Adults Only.

THE MAKING OF EDDIE MURPHY: DELIRIOUS

- "I deeply regret any pain all this has caused. Just like the rest of the world, I am more educated about AIDS in 1996 than I was in 1981. I think it is unfair to take the words of a misinformed 21-year-old and apply them to an informed 35-year- old man. I know how serious an issue AIDS is the world over. I know that AIDS isn't funny. It's 1996 and I'm a lot smarter about AIDS now." (Rubin 1996) – Eddie Murphy (Actor/Writer)
- "It's the stories he tells about his family and his childhood--chasing the ice cream truck, playing the "Fart Game" in the bathtub, his mother throwing her shoes, the family barbeques--that inspire the most raucous laughter." (Rich 2007) – DVD Talk
- "And a lot of the material about gay people and other groups feels, well, uncomfortable. It isn't the majority of the set, but it does make you wince once in a while. And not in a good way." (Musgrove 2009) – IGN

Eddie Murphy: Delirious was recorded live at the DAR Constitution Hall in Washington, D.C. in 1983 and aired on HBO later that year (*The Washington Post* 2015). An album of the same special titled *Eddie Murphy: Comedian* won Eddie Murphy's only Grammy to date at the 26th Annual Grammy Awards in 1984 (Grammy Awards n.d.). Eddie Murphy's other Grammy nominations were from the 25th Annual Grammy Awards in 1985 for Best Comedy Recording (Eddie Murphy (Album)) and Best R&B Instrumental Performance ("Boogie In Your Butt (Instrumental Version") (Single).

REVIEW

Produced as a stand-up special for HBO when Eddie Murphy was still a cast member on *Saturday Night Live*, *Eddie Murphy: Delirious* stands out as capturing how electric a comedian Eddie was when he was only 22 years old. Donning a now iconic tight red leather jacket, Eddie effortlessly launches between stories of him as a kid, celebrity impersonations, and thoughts on himself as a sex symbol without ever breaking much of a sweat.

Director Bruce Gowers opens the special with some documentary footage of Eddie Murphy on the road as The BusBoys perform "(The Boys Are) Back in Town") in the background. In a weird coincidence, the next year their similar number "Cleanin' Up the Town" would appear in *Ghostbusters* (1984), a film Eddie Murphy turned down (Eddie's part was rewritten and trimmed down, eventually going to Ernie Hudson instead).

The documentary footage is fast and loose with Eddie joking to the pilot of a private jet that if he crashes, his name will be all over Eddie's obituary in the paper. Once wishes there were a bit more of this behind-the-scenes material but, understandably, the stand-up set is the star of the show here.

So much has been written about *Eddie Murphy: Delirious* that's it's hard to nail down the highlights. Eddie Murphy's ice cream truck routine is legendary for taking a universal topic and then taking audiences down avenues they'd never think he was going with it. Not unlike *South Park* would prove time and time again years later, it showed how little kids are often selfish jerks to great comedic effect. The bits about his family are often the strongest material on display here whether it's him and his brother Charlie in the bathtub or his mother tossing a shoe with deadly accuracy.

Although Eddie Murphy has routines in here about AIDS and gays that he later apologized for, within the context of the stand-up special, the jokes mostly work. No matter how much Eddie cusses, there's a sweetness and a kind heart to much of the material here that lets a lot of the material slide. Great humor should not play it safe, and Eddie's on a roll the entire time here! Could one get away with some of these jokes now? Probably not, but this special is also over 40 years old by now. The historical context of when and why the jokes were said (keep in mind, Eddie Murphy is only in his early 20s here) are important when critiquing them instead of taking jokes out of context and presenting them ad hoc to a modern audience purely for shock value.

Easily Eddie Murphy's best stand-up material to date, *Eddie Murphy: Delirious* is worth a watch any day of the week.

Eddie Murphy: Raw (1987)

(1987; Paramount Pictures) Director: Robert Townsend; Producer: Robert D. Wachs, Keenen Ivory Wayans; Cinematographer: Ernest R. Dickerson; Written by: Eddie Murphy, Keenen Ivory Wayans; Editor: Lisa Day; Cast: Birdie M. Hale, Leonard Jackson, Samuel L. Jackson, Gwen McGee, Warren Morris, Eddie Murphy, Deon Richmond, Basil Wallace.

Catch him in the act.

THE MAKING OF EDDIE MURPHY: RAW

- "I was a young guy processing a broken heart, you know, kind of an asshole." (Zinoman 2019) – Eddie Murphy (Actor/ Writer)
- "What I supplied was the objective eye. As he was working out material, I gave him notes like, hey, try this, try that... It was much more of that, not, here's your jokes!" (Television Academy Foundation n.d.) – Keenen Ivory Wayans (Writer)
- "It's impossible to deny the virtuosity of his non-stop delivery, but the relentless macho onslaught sadly lacks the saving grace of Richard Pryor's self-irony. Even if Murphy doesn't mean what he says (and he probably does), laughs are forestalled by the feeling that it's all too mechanically manipulative." (Andrew 2012) – *Time Out*
- "However, profanity is a pretty unremarkable quality these days; the country's preoccupation with expletives probably having crested with the Nixon tapes a decade ago, Murphy's obscenity seems more quaint than offensive. No, the rawness of Eddie Murphy is the unfinished kind–unripened, unseasoned, even puerile." (Sheehan, Little Boy Blue 1988) – *The Chicago Reader*

Eddie Murphy: Raw opened domestically on December 18-20, 1987, in 1st place, beating out a crowded weekend around the holidays (Box Office Mojo n.d.). New releases which included the suburban science-fiction comedy **batteries not included* (1987) (4th place), the Goldie Hawn and Kurt Russell romantic comedy *Overboard* (1987) (7th place), and the Bill Cosby alleged comedy *Leonard Part 6* (1987) (10th place).

REVIEW

Instead of opening *Eddie Murphy: Raw* with documentary footage, director Robert Townsend decides to go for a sketch featuring a young Eddie Murphy telling dirty jokes to his increasingly shocked family. Featuring a strong cast including Samuel L. Jackson as his uncle (the rapid-fire dialogue here reminds one of Eddie Murphy's dinner scene with the Klumps years later in his remake of *The Nutty Professor*), this sketch gets things off to a good start.

Eddie Murphy is four years older here than in *Eddie Murphy: Delirious* and is more of a movie star this time around, preening with confidence. Unfortunately, he's also more bitter and angry, going after women wanting him for just his money and fame in several of his jokes.

That's not to say there's not great material in *Eddie Murphy: Raw*. An early joke about Eddie Murphy getting chastised by Bill Cosby for having too dirty of an act is one of the best in his whole set. Murphy's Cosby imitation is flawless (he did Cosby back in his *Saturday Night Live* days), but what really sells it is Murphy knows there's more to his comedy than his cursing. It's both a joke on how well-meaning advice can still hurt, and how different comics have their own unique comic stylings.

Another great bit is about his mother cooking a burger that rivals McDonald's. On paper, it might sound like nothing special, but Murphy's delivery, specific detail (his mother used green bell pepper and onion in the meat, making it sound more meatloaf than burger), and timing makes it measure up to the best material from *Eddie Murphy: Delirious*.

Much of the anti-woman material, while often funny, drags on for too long and feels mean for the sake of it. Unlike Eddie's best material, there's little satire here. It feels like Eddie is nursing a grudge instead of performing finely-honed bits.

A solid stand-up special, although it's not as hilarious as *Eddie Murphy: Delirious*, *Eddie Murphy: Raw* delivers the laughs some of the time. It has a cute opening sketch and is still funnier than most stand-up specials you'll watch in your lifetime.

Right before the COVID-19 pandemic broke out, Eddie Murphy was rumored to be preparing a new stand-up comedy tour that also would have involved him performing some original music. Whether Eddie ever does another stand-up special again, one can only hope. It's been a long time coming, and his stellar Emmy Award-winning guest hosting spot on *Saturday Night Live* in 2019 proved he can still make a live audience roll in the aisles. Let's hope we get another stand-up special out of him before it's too late.

The Golden Child (1986)

(1986; Paramount Pictures) Director: Michael Ritchie; Producer: Edward S. Feldman, Robert D. Wachs; Screenplay: Dennis Feldman; Cinematographer: Donald E. Thorin; Editor: Richard A. Harris; Music: Michel Colombier; Cast: Randall 'Tex' Cobb, Charles Dance, James Hong, Charles Levin, Charlotte Lewis, Eddie Murphy, J.L. Reate, Victor Wong.

Eddie Murphy is the chosen one.

THE MAKING OF THE GOLDEN CHILD

- "But my pictures make their money back: No matter how I feel, for instance, about *The Golden Child* – which was a piece of shit – the movie made more than $100 million. So who am I to say it sucks?" (Zehme 1989) – Eddie Murphy (Actor)
- "We're not doing a *Saturday Night Live* takeoff of ninja pictures. So, again, we're putting Eddie Murphy, the most unreal possible character for this world, into the world and making him believe it. And again, who's the focus character? Eddie Murphy. And we have to see it through his eyes, but he believes it!" (Director's Guild of America n.d.) – Michael Ritchie (Director)
- "The character was villainous, but he was a comic villain as far as I was concerned, and I hadn't done a film like that before. I don't think as an actor you should back off from any experience, so I thought, 'OK, we'll try this.'" (Zemler 2016) – Charles Dance (Actor)
- "In Hollywood they almost force movie stars to become 600-pound gorillas, and there's every reason to believe Murphy has put on some avoirdupois. Needless to say, in

any dispute between a journeyman director and Paramount's most bankable asset, there's no mistaking where the studio would stand. They'd rather see Murphy grow into what he has every intention of becoming -- the Sylvester Stallone of comedy." (Attanasio 1986) – *The Washington Post*

- "But from the moment Murphy appears on the screen, he makes the movie all his own; the special effects are basically just comic props. Murphy slides through the picture with easy wisecracks and unflappable cool, like a hip Bob Hope." (Ebert, *The Golden Child* 1986) – *The Chicago Sun-Times*

During its opening weekend of December 12-14, 1986, *The Golden Child* opened in 1st place. It bested the two other new releases that weekend, *Three Amigos!* (1986), another comedy starring *Saturday Night Live* veterans, and *Crimes of the Heart* (1986), a drama starring Jessica Lange and Sissy Spacek.

REVIEW

Taking a page from Indiana Jones, *The Golden Child* places street-smart Chandler Jarrell (Eddie Murphy) into an unlikely adventure that takes him all the way to Tibet in order to save The Golden Child (J.L. Reate) from a demonic cult. Kee Nang (Charlotte Lewis) feels Murphy is the chosen one from a prophecy who can save the earth from an apocalyptic fate.

In a way, *The Golden Child* feels like two different films. It opens in Los Angeles where Chandler gets up to a lot of his familiar *Beverly Hills Cop*-style schtick investigating the Tibetan locals who are trying to see if he has the goods or not to go on an epic quest. There's nice chemistry between Murphy and Lewis; Dennis Feldman's screenplay lets them go tit for tat in their verbal exchanges, adding some fun tension to their relationship.

As the film moves onto Tibet, it shifts more into action and mysticism which doesn't quite work as well. The fish out of water concept could have been played up a lot more than it is, resulting in action sequences packed with special effects that come off as a little flat at times.

All that being said, J.L. Reate as The Golden Child does a marvelous job. It's an almost silent film performance as she gives a knowing look or conjures up some magic to help guide Chandler on his quest. Charles Dance (*Godzilla: King of the Monsters* (2019), *Last Action Hero* (1993)) has fun taunting Eddie Murphy as the devilish Sardo Numspa.

The best scene in the movie is where Eddie Murphy has to venture alone into a special room to get a legendary knife. It feels a bit like a video game; he has to solve some puzzles and cross a large pit while making wisecracks to calm his nerves down. Too many of the other action scenes, particularly in the third act, are full of gore and explosions and lack the mysticism and humor of the knife sequence.

The Golden Child flounders the most when it tries to appeal to adults and kids. Sometimes, there are a few sexually-charged innuendos. Other times, there's a Pepsi can that transforms into a stop-motion humanoid figure that feels like an outtake from a California Raisins special.

An often fun, if sometimes a bit rote, adventure comedy, *The Golden Child* is an Eddie Murphy effort that's often more silver than gold.

Life (1999)

(1999; Universal Pictures) Director: Ted Demme; Producer: Brian Grazer, Eddie Murphy; Screenplay: Robert Ramsey & Matthew Stone; Cinematographer: Geoffrey Simpson; Editor: Jeffrey Wolf; Music: Wyclef Jean; Cast: Anthony Anderson, Ned Beatty, Lisa Nicole Carson, R. Lee Ermey, Sanaa Lathan, Martin Lawrence, Bernie Mac, Eddie Murphy.

Share it with someone you love.

THE MAKING OF LIFE

- "This movie has more poignancy than the usual Eddie Murphy or Martin Lawrence movies. It has a more developed story... It's a richer production, it's not as predictable, you know?" (H. Thompson n.d.) – Eddie Murphy (Actor)
- "Our mission with the score was to match the music with the decade. I asked 'Clef to take me back to those time periods and make me feel that music, but subtly, so we don't lose the kids of today." (Sinclair 1999) – Ted Demme (Director)
- "It's such much more difficult to do a progressive age makeup, and there's a lot of that involved in *Life*. It's very tough. It's not just creating a character. There has to be a continuity and a visual progression." (H. Thompson, Life (1999) Rick Baker Makeup Featurette n.d.) – Rick Baker (Special Makeup Effects Artist)
- "Murphy breaks into comic riffs now and again but is mostly held in check by director Ted Demme, who, in *Monument Ave.* and *The Ref*, also guided comedian Denis Leary to his only great screen performances." (Baumgarten, Life 1999) – *The Austin Chronicle*

- "The movie doesn't care much about realism, depicting the rigors of prison-farm life about as convincingly as "Life Is Beautiful" portrays a Nazi death camp. But it makes up in energy what it lacks in authenticity, especially when Murphy and Lawrence are in high gear." (Sterritt 1999) – *The Christian Science Monitor*

In its opening domestic box office weekend of April 16-18, 1999, *Life* opened in 1st place (Box Office Mojo n.d.). It beat out *The Matrix* (1999), which had held the 1st place spot for the last 2 weeks in a row.

REVIEW

Movies starring two tip-top comedians are nothing new, but *Life* has the balls to use a period setting to tell a prison story spanning decades about how two friends get a life sentence for a crime they didn't commit. While this doesn't sound like a concept for a comedy, and indeed *Life* has its dramatic moments, the clever scenarios and banter between stars Eddie Murphy and Martin Lawrence (*Big Mommas: Like Father, Like Son* (2011), *Wild Hogs* (2007)) make this work in spite of itself.

After receiving life sentences for a murder they were framed for, Ray Gibson (Eddie Murphy) and Claude Banks (Martin Lawrence) keep trying to escape over the decades to no avail until they hatch one final plan. Along the way, they become either closer or more distant to each other depending on the darkly humorous circumstances they get into.

There's a bittersweet nature to how *Life*'s story unfolds with the main characters never being able to catch a break; even if they do, it never seems to last for long. Eddie Murphy and Martin Lawrence work as a kind of a riff on *The Odd Couple* (1968) with Eddie being more of a fast talker and Martin being more restrained. Whether it's arguing about who gets the cornbread or how to hatch their latest escape, the two play off each other beautifully.

Rick Baker really outdoes himself on the aging makeup here making the two leads get older over time without looking like they stepped out of a *Looney Tunes* short. There's real subtle work being done here with prosthetics that match the more serious overtones of the story.

Plenty of strong character actors play smaller parts here including Ned Beatty (*He Got Game* (1998), *Network* (1976)), Nick Cassavetes (*The Astronaut's Wife* (1999), *Sins of the Night* (1993)), and R. Lee Ermey (*Dead Man Walking* (1995), *The Texas Chainsaw Massacre: The Beginning* (2006)). Even though some of the casting of music artists can feel a bit like stunt casting with names like Heavy D and Rick James, they all play characters and work well in the ensemble while never calling attention to themselves. Obba Babatundé (*Black Dynamite* (2009), *John Q* (2002)) plays Willie Long in an understated manner that nonetheless lets viewers know he's a convict who means business.

Although the picaresque nature of the escapades running throughout *Life* can make for a running time that isn't exactly brisk, the variety of the scenarios makes for a winning movie. One can tell Eddie Murphy and Martin Lawrence are taking their performances seriously here, and it pays off in the mutual respect, albeit begrudgingly at times, the characters have for each other.

An overlooked 1990s comedy with dramatic elements, *Life* is worth tracking down the next time you want a comedy with a little something extra.

Mr. Church (2016)

(2016; Freestyle Releasing) Director: Bruce Beresford; Producers: David Buelow, Mark Canton, Lee Nelson, Courtney Solomon; Screenplay: Susan McMartin; Cinematographer: Sharone Meir; Editor: David Beatty; Music: Mark Isham; Cast: Thom Barry, Natalie Coughlin, Lucy Fry, Christian Madsen, Natascha McElhone, Eddie Murphy, Britt Robertson, Xavier Samuel.

You can always find your way back home.

THE MAKING OF MR. CHURCH

- "[Mr. Church] wasn't a comedy, so there wasn't an expectation on my part. Usually my performance is the engine of the movie, and I have to be funny. But here, I was just a character." (Hunt 2016) – Eddie Murphy (Actor)
- "[Eddie Murphy] has a warm personality. He used to show me films that meant a lot to him, and they were always beautiful films." (TV n.d.) – Bruce Beresford (Director)
- "I wrote the movie because I really wanted to tell the story of this friendship that I experienced that meant the world to me. The process of writing it was really quick but getting it made took a really long time... It took forever to get made and then we shot it in 22 days… There's a movie about the making of this movie." (Gold Derby 2016) – Susan McMartin (Screenwriter)
- "[Eddie Murphy] doesn't seem quite right for the role [of Mr. Church] at first, his blazing charisma ostensibly at odds with his character's unassuming, dignified demeanor. But he tamps it down just enough to be fully plausible, and he adds quiet grace notes, both comic and dramatic, that make his Mr. Church just as captivating for us as he is for the people around him." (Scheck 2016) – *The Hollywood Reporter*

- "*Mr. Church* is a straight-up tear-jerker, bookended by episodes of not one but two fatal diseases and other vicissitudes, particularly pertaining to the travails of single motherhood. The characters have few outside connections — no family members appear and few friends — and so the whole thing seems to take place within a tightly circumscribed bubble. Get out your handkerchiefs, but don't expect to believe a minute of this vastly improbable tale." (Andersen 2016) – *The Seattle Times*

Mr. Church, in a few hundred theaters, opening in 25th place in the domestic box office the weekend of September 16-18, 2016 (Box Office Mojo n.d.). Other major new releases that weekend included *Blair Witch* (2016), the third film in the iconic found footage horror series, *Bridget Jones's Baby* (2016), the third film in the iconic romantic comedy series, and *Snowden* (2016), a biopic from the iconic director Oliver Stone.

REVIEW

Screenwriter Susan McMartin spent a decade trying to get *Mr. Church* made as a movie. Inspired by her experiences growing up the titular family cook, this melodramatic yet moving story shows Eddie Murphy playing a dramatic role with such skill that one wonders how his career might have been different if he hadn't been pegged for comedies so early on in his career.

After her mother dies, Charlie (Britt Robertson) continues to be raised by Mr. Church (Eddie Murphy). While he only tidies up around the house and cooks all their meals, their relationship turns into one of a family of sorts when Charlie goes off to college. After getting pregnant, she returns home as a single mom and raises her child Izzy with none other than Mr. Church.

One of the more intriguing things about this film is how it only offers glimpses of Mr. Church's life outside of what he does for Charlie. Church is a private man, and he is revealed to be a pianist with a troubled past in a way that isn't spelled out for viewers. Bruce Beresford (*Double Jeopardy* (1999), *Driving Miss Daisy* (1989)) shoots the film in a warm glow, adding heart to what is a moving drama. Britt Robertson (*A Dog's Purpose* (2017), *White Rabbit* (2013)) plays Charlie over different stages of her life and manages to convey an effective emotional arc as her character grows up.

Any time the movie strays from the core narrative of Charlie and Mr. Church, it doesn't do as well. Moments when Charlie helps out recovering alcoholic Eddie Larson (Christian Madsen) feel like something out of a lesser Lifetime movie. Earlier scenes with Natalie Coughlin playing the younger Charlie can be t a touch precious, but they work in setting up how much she takes Mr. Church for granted at the start of the film.

It's a nice touch the movie doesn't end after Mr. Church dies of natural causes. Seeing how his life touched so many people at his funeral is moving. Less so is the cloying narration from Charlie providing a meta moment of how Mr. Church's life inspired Charlie to write her first book, which ends the story on a more selfish note than it should.

A slower paced yet thoughtful drama, *Mr. Church* is the kind of movie that grows on you. Eddie Murphy does real strong work here, and it's nice to see a movie that lets him slow down. The role of Mr. Church was originally developed for Samuel L. Jackson, but the film is all the richer for having Eddie Murphy play the lead instead since he gets a chance to spread his wings in a kind of role he's never offered.

Trading Places (1983)

(1983; Paramount Pictures) Director: John Landis; Producer: Aaron Russo; Screenplay: Timothy Harris & Herschel Weingrod; Cinematographer: Robert Paynter; Editor: Malcolm Campbell; Music: Elmer Bernstein; Cast: Don Ameche, Dan Aykroyd, Ralph Bellamy, Jamie Lee Curtis, Denholm Elliott, Paul Gleason, Kristin Holby, Eddie Murphy.

They're not just getting rich... they're getting even.

THE MAKING OF TRADING PLACES

- "Richard Pryor was my idol when I was young, but I don't want to be like Richard. I want to get the same response he got from the people." (Comedy, Eddie Murphy - *Trading Places* Interview: Cast & Director n.d.) – Eddie Murphy (Actor)
- "That first experience [working with Eddie Murphy] was a pure pleasure. Eddie was young and excited [during *Trading Places*]. He was talented and thrilled to be there with Don and Ralph. I remember them in the back of the Rolls Royce. Ameche mentioned this was his 99th movie and Ralph said it was his 200th movie. Eddie said: "Hey Landis, between the three of us, we've made 300 movies!" (Bland 2023) – John Landis (Director)
- "[We] did a significant amount of research about the commodities market in the early 1980's and concluded that it was a very interesting arena in which to set a movie that's not really about financial markets, but required a narrative device that would drive the story." (Planet Money 2013) – Herschel Weingrod (Screenwriter)
- "This incredible turn of fortune is milked for all it's worth as Aykroyd can only watch as Murphy quickly adapts to the

high life with consummate ease. Both actors revel in their respective parts and veterans Bellamy and Ameche delight as the two scheming brothers whose simple bet results in the most extraordinary chain of events." (Haflidason 2000) – BBC

- "John Landis' direction is deft, but the sparkling performances are the real draw." (Arar 1983) – *The Desert Sun*

On its opening domestic weekend of June 10-12, 1983, *Trading Places* opened in 3rd place behind *Octopussy* (1983), the latest James Bond movie starring Roger Moore. The other only competing comedy was *The Man with Two Brains* (1983) starring Steve Martin which had slid down to 8th place in its 2nd week of release.

REVIEW

Everybody loves a rags to riches story, but *Trading Places* throws revenge and the stock market into the mix making for a truly memorable comedy. Dan Aykroyd's and Eddie Murphy's rapid-fire approach to the dialogue works wonders in creating a lively movie that plays to both of their strengths while culminating in a winning ending. One of John Landis' best films, *Trading Places* is a screwball comedy throwback that is an antidote to the "greed is good" mentality espoused in Oliver Stone's *Wall Street* (1987).

Millionaire brothers Randolph Duke (Ralph Bellamy) and Mortimer Duke (Don Ameche) launch an experiment to flip the standards of living for the struggling Billy Ray Valentine (Eddie Murphy) and the elite Louis Winthrope III (Dan Aykroyd). As Valentine enjoys the upper-class lifestyle, Winthrope is sent to live out on the streets. After finding out the Duke brothers are doing this experiment all over a $1 bet, Valentine and Winthrope join forces to get revenge through commodity market trading.

It's a real treat watching Eddie Murphy enjoy the finer things in life as his character goes through a transformation. Watching Dan Aykroyd (*Crossroads* (2002), *The Blues Brothers* (1980)) struggle as he loses his wealth and status, on the other hand, is a bit tragic; his character really goes through the ringer.

Ralph Bellamy (*Pretty Woman* (1990), *Rosemary's Baby* (1968)) and Don Ameche (*Cocoon: The Return* (1988), *Happy Land* (1943)) work quite well as the conniving Duke brothers, bringing their long history of cinematic experience to their weathered characters. Jamie Lee Curtis (*Terror Train* (1980), *True Lies* (1994)) is also fun as the spunky prostitute Ophelia.

As *Trading Places* winds to a close, there's a lot of exposition for the plot mechanics of trading commodities to set up Valentine and Winthrope's scheme at the end, but it's necessary in order to keep the ending from being confusing. John Landis does a masterful job with suspense as the time ticks down to the closing bell, making the audience really wonder if our heroes are going to be victorious or not.

A hell of a lot of fun, *Trading Places* is both a financial and a social satire of the 1980s while not skimping on the laughs. Similar to another Eddie Murphy film, *The Distinguished Gentleman*, *Trading Places* takes what could be a dry subject and livens it up with effective comedy.

You People (2023)

(2023; Netflix) Director: Kenya Barris; Producers: Kenya Barris, Jonah Hill, Kevin Misher; Screenplay: Jonah Hill & Kenya Barris; Cinematographer: Mark Doering-Powell; Editor: Jamie Nelsen; Music: Daniel Tannenbaum; Cast: David Duchovny, Elliott Gould, Jonah Hill, Sam Jay, Lauren London, Nia Long, Julia Louis-Dreyfus, Eddie Murphy.

Opposites attract, families don't.

THE MAKING OF YOU PEOPLE

- "But Jonah, if you go off script, he's right there with you, and sometimes he'll go, or you got to come with him, and he's funny and smart. It was fun working with him." (Jones 2023) – Eddie Murphy (Actor)
- "We talked about it because Kenya was like, "This was originally written for a guy, but me and Jonah think you can do it." They didn't make me change anything about it so it came up very much how my relationships with my homeboys are. It just felt very natural and at ease. That has a lot to do with the writing. They really captured the essence of a real friendship." (Rodriguez 2023) – Sam Jay (Actress)
- "*You People* was based upon seeing characters that we haven't seen who are the black guy who doesn't want his black daughter to marry a white guy because he feels like he raised a princess." (S. Thompson, Why Kenya Barris Wanted 'You People' To Be His Feature Directorial Debut 2023) – Kenya Barris (Director/Screenwriter)
- "Sadly, Amira isn't as well-drawn as her male counterparts, and her interactions with [Julia Louis-Dreyfus] aren't as pointed as those between Hill and Murphy. Co-writers

Barris and Murphy also tend to fall into didacticism at the expense of actual comedy." (Harr 2023) – *The Houston Press*

- "There is a brief dating montage—trips to sneaker stores and museums, lunch, midday strolls, a few extremely chaste kisses and one single suggestion of sex. But there is little in the way of chemistry, mostly because the couple—particularly Amira—are so shallowly realized as individuals." (Blay 2023) - Jezebel

Aside from a brief, limited theatrical release, Netflix essentially launched *You People* direct to streaming. *You People* clocked 55.65 million hours viewed in its opening viewing window from January 23-29, 2023 (Bell 2023).

REVIEW

Comedies where couples get to meet the parents of their partners are nothing new. *You People* sets things apart by taking a political page from *Guess Who's Coming to Dinner* (1967), using a time-honored scenario to tackle some frank discussions about differences in race and culture. A strong cast helps to anchor this strong romantic comedy.

After a whirlwind romance, Ezra Cohen (Jonah Hill) and Amira Mohammed (Lauren London) get to meet their parents who are Jewish and Nation of Islam, respectively. Things get heated when both of their parents meet. Ezra and Amira try to salvage their relationship in the midst of their families' fractious differences.

In *You People*, Eddie Murphy plays a very different role as Akbar, Amira's father. It's a supporting role, but a meaty one. He gets nice scenes to play against Jonah Hill (*Grandma's Boy* (2006), *The Sitter* (2011)) where he is testing him every step of the way. There's a nice ebb and flow and some good twists to his character that give Eddie something to latch onto.

Jonah Hill and Lauren London (*ATL* (2006), *Madea's Big Happy Family* (2011)) have great chemistry, and it's nice how their relationship takes time to build; it feels more realistic and less fantastical than most romantic comedies. Julia Louis-Dreyfus (*Downhill* (2020), *National Lampoon's Christmas Vacation*) is especially strong at capturing the grandstanding nature of Shelley, Ezra's mother.

Some of the dramatics towards the end of the movie are a bit pat, but the characters and engaging dialogue work so well that one hardly notices. Kenya Barris makes a strong theatrical debut showing off iconic Los Angeles locales in a way that makes the city a character of its own. A detour to Las Vegas for Ezra's bachelor party is fun but not as wild as one might expect it to be given the severe consequences. Perhaps a less obvious location for a bachelor party would have been more inspired.

A pretty strong take on a meet the parents premise, *You People* is more thoughtful than most. A great script and strong cast help to elevate what could have been just another romantic comedy into something that strives for more.

The So-So Gems

A Thousand Words (2012)

(2012; Paramount Pictures) Director: Brian Robbins; Producers: Nicolas Cage, Alain Chabat, Stephanie Danan, Norman Golightly, Brian Robbins, Sharla Sumpter Bridgett; Screenplay: Steve Koren; Cinematographer: Clark Mathis; Editor: Ned Bastille; Music: John Debney; Cast: Cliff Curtis, Ruby Dee, Clark Duke, Allison Janney, Jack McBrayer, Eddie Murphy, Lou Saliba, Kerry Washington.

He only has 1000 words left to discover what matters most.

THE MAKING OF A THOUSAND WORDS

- "I never did anything where more than half of the script I can't talk, that challenge... Then I responded to the message of [*A Thousand Words*], how important words are, how you should be careful what you say!" (HipHollywood n.d.) – Eddie Murphy (Actor)
- "What I try to do is to set up a scene or opportunity with him that I think he'll be able to then bring his gifts to it. That's what I try to do is set a comfort level, put him in a position where he'll hopefully make funny out of it!" – Brian Robbins (Director)
- "[The tree] was like a reflection of Eddie. He and the tree are connected so if you hit the tree, it would hurt Eddie and vice versa. I don't know if it has a personality so much that it has nerve endings." – Clark Duke (Actor)
- "[Eddie Murphy's latest is "A Thousand Words" – an uneven film that can't decide if it wants to be a wacky comedy or a family drama. It fails to do either." (Compton 2012) – *The Bowling Green Daily News*

- "Alas, even Murphy's largely wordless, physically adroit performance can't redeem this tortured exercise in high-concept spiritualist hokum, which suggests a cross between "Liar Liar" and Shel Silverstein's "The Giving Tree," but with more kitsch and gay jokes." (Chang 2012) – *Variety*

A Thousand Words had its first major domestic opening on March 9-11, 2012 (Box Office Mojo n.d.). Opening in 6th place, it fell behind other new releases like *John Carter* and *Silent House* which were in 2nd and 5th place respectively. Given the theme of the movie being leaves falling from a tree, perhaps an autumn release would have been more appropriate.

REVIEW

If nothing else, Eddie Murphy is known for his motormouth, often playing characters that speak a mile a minute whilst not lacking confidence. *A Thousand Words* with its fairytale premise takes this comedic strength away from him, resulting in a film that can be surprisingly earnest and moving despite the cheesy marketing; while, yes, Eddie Murphy has a scene where he sings Chili's "Baby Back Ribs" (a gag that felt old when Mike Myers did it in *Austin Powers: The Spy Who Shagged Me* over a decade prior), that's not what the movie is about.

As a literary agent who will do anything to get a deal, Jack McCall (Eddie Murphy) convinces Dr. Sinja (Cliff Curtis) that he has a book in him. In a perverse bit of revenge, Dr. Sinja turns in a mere 5 pages and somehow causes a Bohdi Tree to grow in McCall's backyard. Flush with 1,000 leaves, one leaf falls off for every word Jack says. If all the leaves fall, both the tree and Jack die.

Despite its morbid premise, *A Thousand Words* is a showcase for Eddie Murphy to act with his body language and his expressive eyes. Although some of the reasons for the tree losing leaves are a bit labored (he drinks too much and sings, he struggles to order at Starbucks), the emotional beats tying Jack to his mother and late father in the third act hit home.

In most other movies, the sentimental moments wouldn't work, but Eddie Murphy has a real commitment to his character here. Clark Duke (*Bad Moms* (2016), *The Last Movie Star* (2017)) as Aaron Wiseberger is good as a sort of dopey assistant trying to cover for Jack a lot; he talks when Murphy can't, which in this movie is quite often.

It's too bad Kerry Washington (*Little Man* (2006), *Miracle at St. Anna* (2008)) doesn't get too much to do playing Eddie Murphy's wife in the movie. Aside from one seduction scene that is a great example of miscommunication gone wrong, she doesn't have much to work with.

A Thousand Words is surprising with its darker elements (divorce and suicide are but a few themes running in this film), but the message that people should be kinder to each other and use their words wisely is a good one. It's a shame the ho-hum marketing buried what should have been a bigger film in his career.

Daddy Day Care (2003)

(2003; Sony Pictures Releasing) Director: Steve Carr; Producers: Matt Berenson, John Davis, Wyck Godfrey; Screenplay: Geoff Rodkey; Cinematographer: Steven Poser; Editors: Christopher Greenbury; Music: David Newman; Cast: Elle Fanning, Jeff Garlin, Anjelica Huston, Jonathan Katz, Regina King, Eddie Murphy, Kevin Nealon, Steve Zahn.

D-Day is coming.

THE MAKING OF DADDY DAY CARE

- "You come and see for breakfast a kid will be having a donut and a soda, then, it's like, 'Oh no!, and the kids are running all over the place!" (Archives n.d.) – Eddie Murphy (Actor)
- "The main problem is that they're only allowed to work a couple of hours a day, and then they have to go to school. So we ended up taking 80 days to shoot the film, when I could probably have done it in 40. So it was a long haul." (Lee 2003) – Steve Carr (Director)
- "My career stalled out, and I found myself stuck at home with a newborn while my wife went back to work. And I was kind of miserable, and misery can be funny if it's happening to someone else, so I thought, 'Maybe I can sell a script about this.'" (Pearlman 2011) – Geoff Rodkey (Screenwriter)
- "When you shoot a movie, you're usually here all day for 12 hours, and you're rolling along. With kids, they got to take their nap and drink their milk." (Videos n.d.) – Steven Zahn (Actor)
- "Until now, I hadn't really considered Murphy's new gig as a child entertainer with an $18 million asking price as much of a burden. But *Daddy Day Care* is a nine-alarm metaphor

for a career sanded down to banality." (Borrelli 2003) – *The Toledo Blade*

- "It's a really sweet film that has something to say about force-feeding our young ones as opposed to letting them just enjoy being children." (*Daddy Day Care* Review 2009) – SBS Australia

On its opening domestic weekend of May 9-11, 2003, *Daddy Day Care* had a strong opening in 2nd place. It beat out a competing kids' movie that just came out the week before, *The Lizzie McGuire Movie* (2003).

REVIEW

Comedies get a lot of mileage over the premise of dads trying to raise rowdy kids the best they can; just look at *Mr. Mom* (1983) or *Parenthood* (1989). *Daddy Day Care* is one of those movies with a premise so simple that it's a wonder a movie hadn't been made with that title before. It doesn't try to spice up the story with gunfights like *Kindergarten Cop* (1990). It's a simple premise, and it stays in its lane. Sometimes, that's enough.

After being laid off from their jobs, Charlie Hinton (Eddie Murphy) and Phil Ryerson (Jeff Garlin) hatch a plan to launch a "Daddy Day Care" as a small business. Helping them is their former co-worker Marvin (Steve Zahn). Hot on their heels are director of social services Dan Kubitz (Jonathan Katz) and head of Chapman Academy Miss Gwyneth Harridan (Anjelica Huston). Zaniness ensues.

A real strength of *Daddy Day Care* is how it shows how chaotic kids can be. Not only do Charlie, Phil, and Marvin have to set up a new business, they have to take care of kids that are not their own. Some of them are even under five-years-old, which leads to some rather funny slapstick.

One bright surprise in the cast is Jonathan Katz (*Are We Done Yet?* (2007), *The Spanish Prisoner* (1997)) as the director of social services. His trademark dry delivery brings a bit of sophistication and suspense to the plot as he marks up every little mistake that the guys need to rectify before the titular *Daddy Day Care* is put out of business. Anjelica Huston (*The Addams Family* (1991), *Manhattan Murder Mystery* (1993)) is also great as a sort of joyless schoolmarm; at times, she seems to be drawing inspiration from her role of the lead baddie in *The Witches* (1990).

Eddie Murphy plays a more realistic character this time around to good effect. His anxiety when he reveals to his wife that he's been laid off is palpable, and yet he has a lot of fun improvising moments with the kids. Jeff Garlin (*RoboCop 3* (1993), *Senseless* (1998)) works as a fine foil, especially when he plays guitar and starts singing to try and entertain the tots to little effect.

Daddy Day Care isn't the most tightly structured movie in the world, but its shaggy dog nature makes it a winning one. Murphy and Garlin are great fun to watch as they improve their business and self-esteem by turning what started as a lark into the dream job they never knew they wanted.

There are movies better than *Daddy Day Care*, but it's a rare film that captures the honest chaos and calamities of raising kids. It's not trying to re-invent the wheel, and, in this case, that's a very good thing indeed.

Harlem Nights (1989)

(1989; Paramount Pictures) Director: Eddie Murphy; Producers: Mark Lipsky, Robert D. Wachs; Screenplay: Eddie Murphy; Cinematographer: Woody Omens; Editors: Alan Balsam, George Bowers; Music: Herbie Hancock; Cast: Danny Aiello, Redd Foxx, Denise Arnez Hines II, Jasmine Guy, Michael Lerner, Eddie Murphy, Richard Pryor, Della Reese.

They're up to something big.

THE MAKING OF HARLEM NIGHTS

- "I'm not a very disciplined writer. I'm good with conceptualizing but I'm not good at writing scripts and shit. And I also don't like the process. I like to perform and be an actor, I don't like all that other shit that y'all do. Y'all can have it, and you do it wonderfully." (SPIN 2020) – Eddie Murphy (Writer/Actor)
- "I originally thought we should shoot in black-and-white, but after researching, I decided to make black skin tones the most essential color in the film and use a limited palette. That would set off and highlight the beautiful skin tones of our cast, which was mostly black. I didn't know what Eddie and Larry Paull and Joe Tompkins would think about this, so I created a color chart to demonstrate my idea. After seeing it, they supported the idea, and it became the basis for the look of the entire picture. In that environment, a few very strong color accents seemed to jump off the screen, but most importantly, the skin tones of the actors dominated each scene." (American Cinematographer 2006) – Woody Omens (Cinematographer)

- "I've done about 10 movie scores myself... I did a movie called *Death Wish*, and that was followed by *Soldier Story*, *Harlem Nights*, Eddie's Murphy's film... From that third film on, it was really [Quincy Jones] that made it possible for me to get my foot in the door of the film scoring business. Either he would suggest me or directors would call him and say, 'Hey Q, what about this guy, Herbie Hancock? What do you think?' Quincy would always give me an A rating and reassure [the studio] that they would be making the right choice by choosing me, and I will be eternally grateful to Quincy Jones because of his compassion for providing that doorway for me to enter this wonderful field." (PBS n.d.) – Herbie Hancock (Composer)
- "Murphy doesn't really seem interested in re-creating the 1930s in an authentic way, however. Like Madonna and the other stars in the recent and even more dreadful *Bloodhounds of Broadway*, he approaches his story more as a costume party in which everybody gets to look great while fumbling through a plot that has not been fresh since at least 1938." (Ebert, *Harlem Nights* 1989) – *The Chicago Sun-Times*
- "Written, produced, directed by and starring Mr. Murphy, *Harlem Nights* is a bloated period piece, brandishing big production values, one or two good performances (notably Pryor and Aiello), the occasional laugh, and a spectacularly duff sub-Sting storyline that doesn't so much climax as go prematurely limp." (Kermode, Harlem Nights 1989 n.d.) – *Time Out*

Harlem Nights opened in 1st place at the domestic box office during its opening weekend on November 17-19, 1989 (Box Office Mojo n.d.). Eddie Murphy's R-rated comedy served as a clever bit of counterprogramming to the mostly family films or dramas opening the same weekend. *Harlem Nights* trounced other major new movies of the weekend, many of which would become classics, including Disney's *The Little Mermaid* (1989), *Steel Magnolias* (1989), *All Dogs Go to Heaven* (1989), and *Prancer* (1989).

REVIEW

After having made hit after hit for Paramount (*48 Hrs.*, *Beverly Hills Cop*, *Coming to America*), Eddie Murphy was given the opportunity to direct his own movie. The resulting motion picture, *Harlem Nights*, is a bit surprising. What could have been another flick where Murphy is yet again a contemporary wise-cracking cop or thief is instead a period piece teaming him up with two comic legends: Redd Fox (*Cotton Comes to Harlem* (1970), *The Name of the Game* (1968)) and Richard Pryor (*Blue Collar* (1978), *Silver Streak* (1976)). *Harlem Nights* is an ambitious movie with some fine moments. It's too bad Eddie Murphy has never directed a movie since.

Set in the late 1930s, *Harlem Nights* focuses on Vernest "Quick" Brown (Eddie Murphy) who was adopted as a child by "Sugar" Ray (Richard Pryor). "Bugsy" Calhoun (Michael Lerner) wants a large cut of the action, but Quick has other plans to ensure him and his friends stay on top in the end.

Harlem Nights' story of one gang trying to steal money from another after being threatened is pretty rote; the plot is not something this movie has going for it. What does work, however, is its harsher tone compared to Murphy's earlier comedies. Characters curse a lot, and the violence is more intense, giving scenes a real sense of danger. Woody Omens' cinematography makes for a lush, inviting world full of smoky dance halls and dangerous alleyways.

Eddie Murphy makes Quick a sexy, confident lead who does more than spout off punchlines; he really drives the story forward. Surprisingly, the feisty Redd Foxx has better comic moments (a running gag on Foxx's poor eyesight lands every time) than a rather hum-drum Richard Pryor. Della Reese (*A Thin Line Between Love and Hate* (1996), *Psychic Killer* (1975)) is a riot as Vera, the club's madam who takes no prisoners. Michael Lerner (*Newsies* (1992), *Vibes* (1988)) is an imposing presence as the gangster Bugsy, making what could be an Italian stereotype into a convincing threat to our heroes.

Harlem Nights' period setting, strong cast, and smoldering cinematography are held back by a standard story that could use a few more laughs and better plot twists. The flick's a cool hang, but any time it gets away from Club Sugar Ray, things often drag to a halt.

Still, *Harlem Nights* holds a lot of promise. The lure of three generations of the top African American actors in one movie is a good one, but *Harlem Nights* doesn't quite hit like it should.

Imagine That (2009)

(2009; Paramount Pictures) Director: Karey Kirkpatrick; Producers: Lorenzo di Bonaventura, Ed Solomon; Screenplay: Ed Solomon & Chris Matheson; Cinematographer: John Lindley; Editor: David Moritz; Music: Mark Mancina; Cast: Thomas Haden Church, Ronny Cox, Eddie Murphy, Nicole Ari Parker, Stephen Root, Yara Shahidi, Martin Sheen, Vanessa Williams.

What if your daughter's imagination...
Was the secret to your success?

THE MAKING OF IMAGINE THAT

- "There's never a part in the movie where you're never not happy. From the time you sit down in the movie theater to the time that you leave, it's non-stop fun. That's happiness, isn't it? Laughter and fuzzy feelings." (ScreenSlam n.d.) – Eddie Murphy (Actor)
- "I inherited this really great script from Ed Solomon and Chris Matheson. It's a great gig, directing, sitting in that chair, telling everyone what to do..." (A. t. TV n.d.) – Karey Kirkpatrick (Director)
- "It was so glorious and wonderful, among the many reasons, getting to work with Eddie. Being a New Yorker, watching his meteoric rise, wearing the Eddie Murphy button, showing up at the club just trying to get a glimpse of him but not trying to stalk him because I knew this day was coming, and I didn't want to be the crazy fan..." (B. TV n.d.) – Vanessa Williams (Actress)
- "But along the way, Murphy and the sparkling Shahidi develop wonderful chemistry, Church gamely steals the

show, and the film's star sings, dances and even freaks out without getting too insufferably over-the-top." (McDonnell 2009) – *The Oklahoman*

- "Eddie Murphy's latest vehicle is partly a celebration of fantasy and partly a plea for fathers to spend more time with their children. But mostly, it's about the stock exchange, a more frequent topic in family entertainment than you might suppose." (Wilson 2009) – *The Age*

Imagine That had a tepid domestic box office opening the weekend of June 12-14, 2009, coming in 6th place. The other major new release, a Tony Scott helmed remake of *The Taking of Pelham* (2009) 123, opened in 3rd place. One wonders if the title *Imagine That* was a bit too bland; when filming, the movie's original title was the more evocative *NowhereLand*, a reference to a lyric in the famous Beatles' song "Nowhere Man."

REVIEW

Inspired by an experience co-writer Ed Solomon had when his young daughter inadvertently helped him with a work problem, *Imagine That* is a family film with a heady premise that gets better after a long setup. There's a decent cast here, and the fun chemistry and imagination on display make this more moving than one would think based on the generic poster and trailer.

As a workaholic divorced dad, Evan Danielson (Eddie Murphy) struggles as a financial advisor when his offerings pale to that of a haughty co-worker Johnny Whitefeather (Thomas Haden Church). After having to raise his daughter Olivia (Yara Shahidi) more than he's used to, he talks to her imaginary friends while playing under her special "goo-gaa" blanket. Wanting to mix business with family, he asks her imaginary friends for stock advice. Improbably, this works, but Olivia starts to feel used.

The conflict between work and family is one seen in many films whether they star Eddie Murphy (*Daddy Day Care*, *The Haunted Mansion*) or not (*Hook* (1991), *Liar Liar* (1997)). A trick director Karey Kirkpatrick uses which is both baffling and brilliant is how the imaginary world of Olivia is never seen by the audience. This even rings true in the final scene where Eddie Murphy sees a dragon fly into the sky; the big visual pay-off is some elegiac floating leaves.

Kirkpatrick's budget-friendly choice to not make the imaginary land a madcap *Roger Rabbit* sort of scenario really makes the audience empathize with Eddie Murphy's character. From his point of view, when Olivia is using her imagination, she is a nutty kid. Both Eddie Murphy and the audience see the reality an adult sees, which is absolutely nothing. This frames the growing relationship between father and daughter as a challenge that takes work; if he saw the same imaginative creatures that she did, there would be little dramatic conflict to the story.

Several scenes of Evan and Olivia playing together work well whether it's Eddie Murphy enacting out the silly voices that Olivia's imaginary friends would understand or dining on a breakfast of pancakes topped with ketchup. The power of play is something adults all too often forget, and it's nice to see the characters bond by being silly. Is he exploiting her so he will do better at work? Absolutely, but the back and forth between the two works as a legitimate form of family bonding up to a point.

Martin Sheen (*Captain Nuke and the Bomber Boys* (1996), *O* (2001)) as the big cheese Dante D'Enzo makes a formidable presence in the climactic meetings where we see if Evan or Johnny gets the promotion at work. It's nice to see Eddie Murphy reunite with Ronny Cox from his *Beverly Hills Cop* days playing a small part as an executive who is mystified by Murphy's success. Thomas Haden Church (*Lone Star State of Mind* (2002), *Tales from the Crypt: Demon Knight* (1995)) is inspired as a manipulative man who leans into his questionable Native American heritage too hard at every opportunity.

Imagine That wouldn't work at all if it wasn't for Yara Shahidi's (*Salt* (2010), *Peter Pan & Wendy* (2023)) grounded performance as Olivia. Despite *Imagine That* being her first movie, she has a warmth and playfulness that brings the movie to life. If she didn't believe in her imaginary world, the audience wouldn't either.

Much of the soundtrack comprises of Beatles covers with varying effectiveness. *I Am Sam* (2001) did this same kind of thing to better effect almost a decade prior. The use of so many Beatles songs in *Imagine That* comes off as suckering in Boomers with nostalgia more than being central to the narrative.

One of Eddie Murphy's more unique family films, *Imagine That* uses the quirkiness of its premise to its advantage. In lesser hands, this would have been a forgettable piece of fluff. Instead, it's a clever if not sometimes overbaked feature that combines schmaltz with the stock market. It's a damn shame Karey Kirkpatrick hasn't directed a live-action film since.

Holy Man (1998)

(1998; Buena Vista Pictures Distribution) Director: Stephen Herek; Producers: Roger Birnbaum, Stephen Herek; Screenplay: Tom Schulman; Cinematographer: Adrian Biddle; Editor: Trudy Ship; Music: Alan Silvestri; Cast: James Brown, Jon Cryer, Morgan Fairchild, Jeff Goldblum, Robert Loggia, Dan Marino, Eric McCormack, Eddie Murphy.

God's Gift to Home Shopping.

THE MAKING OF HOLY MAN

- "I did this horrendous film once, [James Brown] did a cameo in it... A movie called *Holy Man*. It was not that bad, but it was pretty bad... He told me, 'You should do my life story!' 'Well,' I said, 'people would be laughing!' He was like, 'No, no, they'd be laughing if you were playing around with me. If they'd see it, people would be takin' it serious. You got all that in-between stuff!', whatever that means!" (Shows n.d.) – Eddie Murphy (Actor)
- "[*Holy Man*] was great fun. A smorgasbord of laughs. Eddie Murphy does a hilarious imitation of me. Stephen Herek, the director who did *Mr. Holland's Opus* has a great heart, and this movie is not without its warm romance. The laughs were also helped by a writer, Mitch Glazer, who came in and worked on the script and is terrifically talented." (Edrive 1998) – Jeff Goldblum (Actor)
- "*Holy Man* features (1) Eddie Murphy as (2) a self-styled spiritual pilgrim who drifts into the lives (3) of a couple of hustling home-shopping-network execs and heals their souls, (4) imparting viewers with a Life Lesson. Yet what remains infinitely unknowable about this unholy dud is how

all attempts at comedy and spiritual uplift got shot to hell."
(Schwarzbaum, Holy Man 1998) – *Entertainment Weekly*

- "Written by Tom Schulman (*8 Heads In A Duffel Bag*, *Second Sight*) and directed by Stephen Herek (*Critters*, *Don't Tell Mom The Babysitter's Dead*), *Holy Man* begins as a satire of the tacky consumerism of home-shopping networks, but shifts gears about halfway through to become a simplistic morality tale. As satire, it's obvious and tame, and as a cautionary tale, it's glib and hypocritical." (Rabin 2002) – *AV Club*

On its opening domestic box office weekend of October 9-11, 1998, *Holy Man* debuted in 5th place (Box Office Mojo n.d.). The only other new major release that same weekend was *One Tough Cop* (1998) starring Stephen Baldwin, which opened in 13th place.

REVIEW

In the 1980s and 1990s, there was a raft of home-shopping network channels, QVC being chief among them. Coincidentally, there were also evangelists preaching on TV asking their parishioners to send them money. *Holy Man* tries to satirize both targets with varying degrees of success while giving Eddie Murphy a rare supporting role.

After Ricky Hayman (Jeff Goldblum), a manager at the Good Buy Shopping Network, fails to meet his sales quotas, he has a chance encounter with G (Eddie Murphy), a bald mustachioed new-age guru who is nonetheless charismatic. Intrigued, Ricky arranges for G to guest on a segment on his channel and sales go through the roof. As G's life changes due to the rigors of fame, Ricky starts to develop feelings for his work rival Kate Newell (Kelly Preston).

Make no mistake, despite Eddie Murphy being front and center on the posters and in the trailers, *Holy Man* is a Jeff Goldblum (*Adam Resurrected* (2008), *The Favor, the Watch and the Very Big Fish* (1991)) vehicle. Coming hot off his smash hit *Jurassic Park* (1993), Goldblum plays a befuddled albeit charming marketing manager with a dramatic weight nobody else in the cast attempts to match. Eddie Murphy's chaotic good nature is a nice foil to the considerably more mild-mannered Jeff Goldblum.

There's something intriguing to Eddie Murphy's titular *Holy Man* character. He sells products while preaching the tenets of anti-consumerism, and how people should achieve better work-life balance and be kinder to the world. There's a nice message in the screenplay by Tom Schulman (*Dead Poets Society* (1989), *What About Bob?* (1991)), and Eddie Murphy often delivers lines with an honest sincerity that gives the movie a lot of heart. A scene where Q helps a man through his fear of flying manages to be both moving and funny, which is no mean feat.

Holy Man benefits from a fun supporting cast with Robert Loggia (*Big* (1998), *Curse of the Pink Panther* (1983)) standing out for chewing the scenery as John McBainbridge, a boss who's a real battle-axe. What doesn't work with *Holy Man* is the litany of over-the-top celebrity cameos trying to shill products with Q's charm, including but not limited to James Brown (*Doctor Detroit* (1983), *Rocky IV* (1985)), Dan Marino (*Bad Boys II* (2003), *Little Nicky* (2000)), Morgan Fairchild (*Killing Blue* (1988), *Shattered Illusions* (1989)), Florence Henderson (*Dickie Roberts: Former Child Star* (2003), *Shakes the Clown* (1991)), and Soupy Sales (*Birds Do It* (1966), *The Two Little Bears* (1961)).

As *Holy Man* gets more serious at the end, it lays on its messaging a bit too thick. Any emotional payoffs feel forced and like something out of a different movie. One has to wonder if *Holy Man* was written as a drama first that was refined into a comedy later.

Notable for featuring Eddie Murphy in a more toned-down version of his often-impish persona, *Holy Man* has some good ideas with bad execution. This slapdash marketing of the movie (Eddie Murphy with a chainsaw! Morgan Fairchild getting electrocuted!) belies the sometimes-thoughtful aphorisms dropped by Murphy throughout the film. *Holy Man* is better than it should be.

Metro (1997)

(1997; Touchstone Pictures) Director: Thomas Carter; Producer: Roger Birnbaum; Screenplay: Randy Feldman; Cinematographer: Fred Murphy; Editor: Peter E. Berger; Music: Steve Porcaro; Cast: Paul Ben-Victor, Carmen Ejogo, Art Evans, Donal Logue, Kim Miyori, Eddie Murphy, Michael Rapaport, Michael Wincott.

Life is a negotiation.

THE MAKING OF METRO

- "I like to be able to do a gritty, macho popcorn movie. This movie gave me the opportunity to play more of a dramatic role than I've ever played before. I've never played anything this heavy." (Carter n.d.) – Eddie Murphy (Actor)
- "I should have made a PG-13 movie, it would have made a lot more money. We gave Eddie free reign. He was very funny, but every other word was some profane word. I was laughing. At the same time, I'm going, 'Are we going a little too far here? Maybe we should tone it down!'" (Kluger n.d.) – Thomas Carter (Director)
- "Still, the extended central action sequence, in which Roper and McCall, riding in an old Caddy convertible, chase a cable car that Korda has commandeered and inadvertently accelerated, is outstanding. It also affords Roper the opportunity to transcend physical heroics and vie for savior status. But then, Roper as a superman is built into the whole enterprise." (Feinstein 1997) – *Variety*
- "*Metro* feels like Carter borrowed a paint-by-numbers set from action director Michael Bay (*Bad Boys, The Rock*) and filled in only the explosions and car chases. But even

those are sloppy -- especially to Bay Area movie goers." (Blackwelder n.d.) – *Spliced Wire*

Upon opening on Martin Luther King Jr. weekend in January 17-20, 1997, *Metro* came in 2nd place at the domestic box office. It was beat out by *Beverly Hills Ninja*, a comedy-action film from another *SNL* alum, Chris Farley.

REVIEW

Metro came out at an interesting time in Eddie Murphy's career. After two rated-R comedies that didn't set the world on fire (*Beverly Hills Cop III* and *Vampire in Brooklyn*), the action-heavy *Metro* was Murphy's last go at an R-rated movie until *Dolemite Is My Name* dropped on Netflix 22 years later. Murphy was about to step into a world of more family-oriented comedies, and *Metro* was an inadvertent farewell to the cop capers that started his cinematic career.

Inspector Scott Roper (Eddie Murphy), a hostage negotiator with a steely resolve to match his improvisational approach to assignments, is assigned a new partner. He's assigned to Kevin McCall (Michael Rapaport), a jittery newbie who is more by the book. After investigating the jewel thief duo of Michael Korda (Michael Wincott) and Clarence Teal (Paul Ben-Victor), Roper's superior, Lieutenant Sam Baffert (Art Evans), gets killed. Roper and McCall have to track them down through the streets of San Francisco. In addition to his stressful work life, Roper is trying to woo back Ronnie Tate (Carmen Ejogo), a former flame who has had enough of his trademark bullshit.

Aside from a tepid opening scene where Murphy distracts a bank robber with a bag of donuts that feels like a deleted scene from *Beverly Hills Cop II*, the action in *Metro* is often quite exciting. Fans of car chases, explosions, and hostage negotiations will enjoy the meaty sequences making up the back half of the film. The final showdown at a shipyard features a trap that wouldn't be out of place in a *Saw* movie!

Director Thomas Carter focuses on getting great performances from the actors which elevates the mostly tired narrative. There is a noted commitment to the dramatic acting here; nobody's going through the motions. Everybody from Carmen Ejogo (*Alien: Covenant* (2017), *Love's Labour's Lost* (2000)) as the cautious yet bubbly romantic interest to Michael Wincott (*The Sicilian* (1987), *The*

Three Musketeers (1993)) as the super-intense baddie plays their roles with enough flair so you don't forget them after the credits roll.

It's the comedic scenes between the action that really take things down. It's not that they aren't funny (Murphy flirting with Ejogo about why you have to say "nekkid in Tahiti" is amusing), but they feel out of place with the rather bloody and violent action scenes and moody cinematography. If you're going for a straight action movie with violent kills, stick to the assignment and stop reminding the audience of *Beverly Hills Cop* every other scene.

Metro's generic title doesn't help things either. The word "metro" can mean many things: a city, the subway system in Washington D.C., or even a snappy fashion style. What *Metro* does not describe well is the very nature of this movie, a bit of a hidden gem in Eddie Murphy's filmography.

Norbit (2007)

(2007; Paramount Pictures) Director: Brian Robbins; Producer: John Davis, Eddie Murphy; Screenplay: Eddie Murphy & Charlie Murphy; Jay Scherick & David Ronn; Story: Eddie Murphy & Charlie Murphy; Cinematographer: Clark Mathis; Editor: Ned Bastille; Music: David Newman; Cast: Terry Crews, Cuba Gooding Jr., Eddie Griffin, Eddie Murphy, Thandiwe Newton, Lindsey Sims-Lewis, Marlon Wayans, Katt Williams.

Have you ever made a really big mistake?

THE MAKING OF NORBIT

- "Originally, [*Norbit*] wasn't a multiple character thing. It was something me and an actress were going to do. It was dark, there was a lot of violence and fighting. It was dark like *Death to Smoochy* or *Throw Momma from the Train* or something. I said, 'Wait a minute! What if I play the woman?' It kind of diffuses… It's one thing for me to put a woman in a body bag and hit it with a shovel, and it's another thing to put myself in a body bag and hit it with a shovel, you know? The second one is funnier!" (fevercity n.d.) – Eddie Murphy (Writer/ Actor)
- "Mr. Wong is the most challenging. Mr. Wong's appliances are made out of silicone. Silicone has the advantage that you can intrinsically color it, and it's a translucent material. So we actually sculpted that makeup. Just doing the sculpture and life cast over Eddie takes about a month!" (ingmarlaraTV n.d.) – Rick Baker (Special Effects Makeup Artist)
- "When I went to talk about [*Norbit*], the first draft I read was way darker. It was about this woman fucking abusing this guy. I think it was always supposed to be a comedy, but you

can imagine how twisted that would be. That's why I wanted to do it. And then it just got very … I don't know how to describe it … It's like it turned into a kind of Baskin-Robbins commercial. Eddie was hardly ever there, which was really sad. He has the best stand-ins you've ever seen. Literally, from five feet away, you would think they were Eddie. I think I probably did most of the movie with his stand-ins." (Jung 2020) – Thandiwe Newton (Actress)

- "There's an 80-year-old Asian man called Mr. Wong, I actually treated him differently. He was brittle and I talked to him differently than when he was Rasputia, a big 450 lb. mean woman. I treated her differently. And then when he was Norbit, it was a whole other thing. It was like acting with three different people completely!" (McLeod 2007) – Terry Crews (Actor)

- "Unlike the female characters Murphy portrayed in *The Nutty Professor* and its sequel – the nurturing Mama Klump and the perpetually horny Granny Klump – Rasputia is purposely one-dimensional in the way she terrorizes her dweeb husband, Norbit (Murphy again), and everyone else within distance. (Even children and dogs aren't safe around her.)" (Davis 2007) – *The Austin Chronicle*

- "[*Norbit*] is Murphy doing what he does best, genial cruelty and good-natured nastiness. His comedy is so obvious that he dares the audience to see every moment coming and then delivers by topping expectations and making his jokes bigger and more ridiculous than anyone could imagine. You've heard of rapier wit. This is sledgehammer wit, wielded with sledgehammer precision." (LaSalle 2007) – *The San Francisco Chronicle*

On its opening domestic box office weekend of February 9-11, 2007, *Norbit* opened in 1st place (Box Office Mojo n.d.). It beat out the other major new release of the weekend, *Hannibal Rising*

(2009), a prequel to the cannibal mastermind villain made famous in *Manhunter* (1986), *Silence of the Lambs* (1991), and *Hannibal* (2001).

REVIEW

Norbit is the first time Eddie Murphy has been credited for writing one of his movies in over a decade since 1995's *Vampire in Brooklyn*. On the surface, it has hallmarks of some of his past hits: Eddie playing multiple characters in detailed prosthetics, broad physical comedy, and a romantic love interest at the center giving the movie some heart. In practice, *Norbit* has a darker story at its core which leads to a sometimes uneasy but also shockingly sweet comedy.

While being raised in an orphanage that's also a Chinese restaurant, young Norbit (Khamani Griffin) and Kate (China Anderson) strike up a friendship before Kate gets adopted and moves away. A few years later, Norbit feels indebted to Rasputia (Lindsey Sims-Lewis) after she rescues him from bullies. Now a middle-aged man married to Rasputia (Eddie Murphy), Norbit (Eddie Murphy) is surprised to see Kate (Thandiwe Newton) come back into his life. However, Kate is engaged to Deion (Cuba Gooding Jr.). Norbit must decide if he is to leave his abusive wife and pursue his childhood crush or to stay the course.

These characters aren't as cardboard cutout as they might seem from the commercial. It's nice to see how Norbit gains confidence over the film as he frees himself from a marriage that feels like it was a form of entrapment to begin with. Thandiwe Newton gives Kate a real sweetness to her character which is needed to counter the aggressiveness of Rasputia.

As he tends to do every so often in his comedies, Eddie Murphy plays multiple characters in the film: Norbit, Rasputia, and Mr. Wong. Norbit is a warmer take on the nerdy Kit character Murphy played to such good effect in *Bowfinger*. Rasputia is a highlight with her attitude being more of a force of nature that spells trouble whenever she's onscreen. Mr. Wong is underrated as a passive-aggressive elderly Chinese man which takes the most advantage of Rick Baker's makeup effects.

As a movie, *Norbit* can feel a bit disjointed at times. Eddie Griffin (*Brain Donors* (1992), *Scary Movie 3* (2003)) and Katt Williams (*The House Next Door: Meet the Blacks 2* (2021), *The Perfect Holiday* (2007)) as recovering pimps Pope Sweet Jesus and Lord Have Mercy, respectively, have a nice chemistry going on that feels awfully truncated. Brian Robbins shoots the film with saturated colors giving everything a cartoon look, which works well with the larger-than-life characters.

While the marketing for *Norbit* focused on Rasputia's catch-phrases and singing "Don't Cha" by The Pussycat Dolls over and over, the film itself is better than the manic trailers suggest. Norbit and Kate have a real sweetness to their lifelong relationship that makes them worth rooting for. The romantic comedy at the heart of *Norbit* is not as flippant as it appears.

Showtime (2002)

(2002; Warner Bros. Pictures) Director: Tom Dey; Producers: Jane Rosenthal, Jorge Saralegui; Screenplay: Keith Sharon, Alfred Gough & Miles Millar; Story: Jorge Saralegui; Cinematographer: Thomas Kloss; Editor: Billy Weber; Music: Alan Silvestri; Cast: Yasiin Bey, Alex Borstein, Pedro Damian, Judah Friedlander, Robert De Niro, Eddie Murphy, Rene Russo, William Shatner.

Lights. Camera. Aggravation.

THE MAKING OF SHOWTIME

- "There's a difference doing action stuff when you're 40 than when you're 25. You take a lot of it home with you. Needless to say, my next movie will be called *The Man in the Chair in his Slippers!*" (Graveyard n.d.) – Eddie Murphy (Actor)
- "[I was] disconnected from the cinematic skill as a cameraman being in a management position. It hadn't been a creative position on that size movie." (British Cinematographer n.d.) – Thomas Kloss (Cinematographer)
- "Oh, [Robert De Niro and Eddie Murphy] were fabulous. We would do the scene as written, then we would do it as not written, then they would do the scene as they saw it, we would do it -- and we did it, and it was great fun. And it's great." (CNN Larry King Live 2002) – William Shatner (Actor)
- "Unlike *Analyze This* or *Meet the Parents*, *Showtime* is a lead-balloon caper, a showcase for the duller side of Bobby D. Murphy, by contrast, might almost be doing a replicant version of his live-wire younger self. His verbal energy, even at its most superficially aggressive, now comes across as an overeagerness to please." (Gleiberman, Showtime 2002) – *Entertainment Weekly*

- "There just might have been a good idea in there about reality television and media distortion, but frankly, it's already been done to much better effect. In any case, *Showtime* is concerned with big-bang action set-pieces set off by comic interludes, certainly not any kind of social statement. That would be fine were the action set-pieces anything other than humdrum, the comic interludes anything other than routine yuks." (K. Jones 2022) – *The Austin Chronicle*

Opening domestically on March 15-17, 2002, *Showtime* opened in 3rd place (Box Office Mojo n.d.). Above it in 1st and 2nd place, respectively, were two movies that would prove to be the first entries in what would become long-running film franchises: *Ice Age* (2002) and *Resident Evil* (2002).

REVIEW

Robert De Niro was on a comedy roll in the late 1990s and early 2000s with comedy franchises teaming him with Billy Crystal (*Analyze This* (1999), *Analyze That* (2002)) and Ben Stiller (*Meet the Parents* (2000), *Meet the Fockers* (2004), *Little Fockers* (2010)). Aiming more for a similar "can't miss" formula, *Showtime* teams up De Niro with none other than Eddie Murphy. Although trailers for this movie were amiable enough (in one scene, William Shatner tells Robert De Niro "That was the worst acting I've ever seen!"), the loose premise doesn't carry enough weight to bear a sketch, let alone a feature film.

After Detective Mitch Preston (Robert De Niro) is filmed breaking a news reporter's camera, he is forced into making a reality show titled "Showtime" to keep his police department from being sued. When Preston stops a staged purse snatching (!) and argues with Trey Sellars (Eddie Murphy), a fast-talking actor who is pretending to be a cop (!!), producer Chase Renzi (Rene Russo) decides to add Trey to their rather impromptu reality show (!!!). Along the way, they have to track down arms dealer Cesar Vargas (Pedro Damian) who foils their every turn.

Showtime's plot takes a while to get in gear thanks to what is one of the most convoluted first acts in recent memory. As the story continues, we see their reality TV show "Showtime" become a hit, but little of the scenes we see being filmed for this show within a movie come across being that funny or outrageous. To add insult to injury, we see precious little of the TV show itself; there could have been some rich satire of how reality shows distort reality to make good television, but *Showtime* is lacking wit and a good many other things.

Eddie Murphy has good energy in a brief sequence where William Shatner (*Big Bad Mama* (1974), *Free Enterprise* (1998)) teaches T.J. Hooker moves to him while Robert De Niro (*Angel Heart*

(1987), *Shark Tale* (2004)) often seems bored. Granted, De Niro's character in this movie is that of a big grump who is meant to lack enthusiasm. His one good scene is where he returns to his apartment to find it decorated to hell with a pet dog to boot in order for his persona to be more appealing for his reality show audience. De Niro's disgust is as palpable as the audience's.

Rene Russo (*Mr. Destiny* (1990), *Outbreak* (1995)) does a yeoman's work as the driven producer of the reality show. Yasiin Bey (*The Hitchhiker's Guide to the Galaxy* (2005), *Where's Marlowe?* (1998)) has some fun scenes as Lazy Boy, a slacker gangster. Less inspired is Pedro Damian (Eagle's Wing (1979), *Paper Boats* (2019)) as the bad guy Cesar Vargas who fails to be a threatening foe. When he tends to coax the movie into action scenes, they always take a bite out of whatever comedy seems to be going on.

A reality show satire of *Cops* could make a good movie, but *Showtime* truly fails to distinguish itself from the dozens of buddy cop movies out there. In particular, a scene late in the film trying to build a bond of real friendship between De Niro and Murphy feels forced something awful. Featuring neither their best nor their worst work, *Showtime* could hardly be called a showcase.

The Adventures of Pluto Nash (2002)

(2002; Warner Bros. Pictures) Director: Ron Underwood; Producers: Shakir Aibani, Martin Bregman, Michael Bregman, Louis A. Stoller; Screenplay: Neil Cuthbert; Cinematographer: Oliver Wood; Editor: Alan Heim, Paul Hirsch; Music: John Powell; Cast: Peter Boyle, John Cleese, Rosario Dawson, Pam Grier, Luis Guzmán, Jay Mohr, Eddie Murphy, Randy Quaid.

The Man on the Moon.

THE MAKING OF THE ADVENTURES OF PLUTO NASH

- "That's challenging: when you're sitting in the screening room and you see the first print of *Pluto Nash*. I remember the first time we watched *Pluto Nash*, I had my son Myles with me. He was probably about 8. Myles is sitting there with me, and the movie's all soft. Then at the end, it goes silent, and my little baby son goes, 'Corny.' That was challenging." (Marchese 2024) – Eddie Murphy (Actor)
- "Eddie was always very pleasant and easy to work with in some regards. But he didn't like the scripts we were writing. He kept rejecting the scripts. And we'd bring on a new writer and try again; and we'd bring on a new writer and try again. And it just...he wasn't responding. I mean, maybe we should have stopped at that point. I don't know. He said that his best work was: a film written for [someone like] Sylvester Stallone or Harrison Ford and he would bring the comedy. And so our last draft was fairly straight. Probably the straightest [of all our drafts]. And it's...I don't know. I feel like Eddie gave a lot. But he didn't...I mean, he wasn't feeling that funny, I don't think." (B. Harris, How Did This Get Made: A Conversation With Ron Underwood, Director

Of 'Tremors,' 'City Slickers,' And 'The Adventures Of Pluto Nash' 2020) – Ron Underwood (Director)

- "It's a lot more fun to be physical, sometimes, in a scene, and go more on instinct and adrenaline rather than thinking about dialogue and relationships and kind of making that work. There's different kind of connections you have to make and movements you have to make during an action sequence, especially when there's blue screen." (TV Guide 2002) – Rosario Dawson (Actress)

- "You usually can't tell when a movie is going to be shit, but on that one you could. And I think Ron Underwood, the director, got victimized by that, because that guy is good. But because of the material and the style in which some players came to work, we were off the mark, you know? A lot of hanky-panky going on there. So, I wasn't surprised. I was surprised it turned out to be better than I thought it was going to be." (Rabin, Joe Pantoliano was in *Risky Business* and *The Sopranos* and has stories to prove it 2012) – Joe Pantoliano (Actor)

- "An abundance of noise, explosions, gunplay, chases, special effects, futuristic eye candy and star power (including John Cleese, Pam Grier and Peter Boyle) generates very little pure fun or excitement in this cluttered visit to the moon." (Halverson 2002) – *The Sacramento News & Review*

- "[Eddie Murphy] has no chemistry whatsoever with leading lady Rosario Dawson (of *Men in Black II*, who deserves much better), as a singer who follows him around for reasons that seem to have been left on the cutting-room floor. Too bad they didn't leave this whole movie there – or didn't just ship what was salvaged to the remainder bin at Blockbuster [Video]." (Lumenick 2002) – *The New York Post*

On its opening domestic weekend on August 16-18, 2002, *The Adventures of Pluto Nash* opened 10th place in the box office (Box

Office Mojo n.d.). The other major new contender for the weekend was the surfing romantic comedy *Blue Crush* (2002) which opened in 3rd.

The Daily Mail described *The Adventures of Pluto Nash*'s plot as a "humdrum stand-up-for-your-property story." In Owen Gleiberman's review of the film for *Entertainment Weekly*, he praised Randy Quaid playing a "bald and towering, with hypno-eyes and a '50s robot voice, as a silver-suited droid."

REVIEW

A rare comedy that's more infamous for its bad reviews than the movie itself, *The Adventures of Pluto Nash* is more aggressively sub-par than anything. It sends Eddie Murphy to a high-concept gangster movie on the moon packed with lasers and explosions, but it also has a central mystery that's so dull that by the time the big plot twist happens, one is too bored to care that much.

After abandoning his smuggler ways to run a nightclub, Pluto Nash (Eddie Murphy) finds himself on the run once again when he refuses an offer from Rex Crater to buy him out. As Nash tries to track down Crater to confront him, he goes on his adventure with creaky android Bruno (Randy Quaid) and lounge singer Dina (Rosario Dawson) tagging along.

The scope of the sets and the future moon-based society in *The Adventures of Pluto Nash* would have been better suited to a science-fiction film like *Blade Runner* (1982). It leaves viewers confused about what can feel like an eternal struggle in lesser Eddie Murphy motion pictures: is this an action or a comedy movie?

At the heart of the story is a central mystery of who is Rex Crater and how can Pluto Nash reach him? As far as hooks go, it's not bad, but when the character of Pluto Nash gives Eddie Murphy next to nothing to work with (he looks bored in just about every scene), the plot loses any momentum it might have had. John Powell's sluggish main *Pluto Nash* theme is a real pantload sounding just a few notes off from Christopher Tyng's funkier *Futurama* theme song.

Thankfully, a few of the supporting roles work. Randy Quaid (*Caddyshack II* (1988), *Hard Rain* (1998)) makes Bruno into a horny retrograde android full of more piss and vinegar than just about anything else in this film. Rosario Dawson (*Kids* (1995), *Shattered Glass* (2003)) is pleasant as Dina, and it's nice to see her actually sing at the end of the movie; at least someone's living their dreams. While he's not in the film that much, Luis Guzmán is a lot of fun as

Pluto Nash super-fan Felix. It's great to see someone excited about Pluto Nash, but we never get a sense as to why everyone else thinks he's the coolest cat in town.

It's only at the end of the film when Eddie Murphy comes alive playing the dastardly cigar-smoking Rex Crater in a mildly surprising reveal. While the battle between Pluto and his clone is not as much fun as it could have been, the movie peps up ever so slightly when Murphy plays Crater with a real swagger tinged with anger. Maybe this movie should have been *The Adventures of Rex Crater* instead?

A sometimes visually impressive caper, *The Adventures of Pluto Nash* is too boring for adults and too humdrum for kids. It's not as bad a movie as its reputation belies, but it would have been more fun if it was.

Tower Heist (2011)

(2011; Universal Pictures) Director: Brett Ratner; Producers: Brian Grazer, Eddie Murphy, Kim Roth; Screenplay: Ted Griffin, Jeff Nathanson, Solomon J. LeFlore; Story: Adam Cooper & Bill Collage, Ted Griffin; Cinematographer: Dante Spinotti; Editor: Mark Helfrich; Music: Christophe Beck; Cast: Casey Affleck, Alan Alda, Matthew Broderick, Judd Hirsch, Téa Leoni, Eddie Murphy, Gabourey Sidibe, Ben Stiller.

Ordinary guys. An extraordinary robbery.

THE MAKING OF TOWER HEIST

- "I had two or three times on the set where I was like, 'You know, technically, this is a stunt!' There's a stunt dude doing over there, but [the director] Brett [Ratner would] be having me doing stuff where afterwards you'd be like, 'That was a stunt. I shouldn't have been doing it!' (TheCelebFactor 2011) – Eddie Murphy (Actor/Producer)
- "I raced to get to the set to shoot Eddie Murphy. And he felt that love. I don't think he felt that from a director in a long time." (Gordon 2011) – Brett Ratner (Director)
- "Realism was an important part of this story. The original plan was to produce *Tower Heist* with the Alexa digital camera, but Brett liked the idea of shooting on film in anamorphic format. We did that except for three night scenes, which we shot with the Alexa camera and Hawk lenses." (British Cinematographer n.d.) – Dante Spinotti (Cinematographer)
- "With every cog in place, you'd think this comedy machine, despite being directed by industry tool Brett Ratner (*Rush Hour 3*), would run smoothly. While the setup works well enough, the heist itself isn't executed on the page with

much imagination. What's left is an amusing team of misfits bumbling around aimlessly in search of a disappointing payoff more ridiculous than naming a humanitarian award after Bernie Madoff." (Martinez, Tower Heist gives Eddie Murphy a comedy vehicle that doesn't crash and burn 2011) – *The San Antonio Current*

- "Eddie Murphy delivers his funniest performance in over 20 years as the only non-amateur of the group, the amped-up street hustler, Slide. The role is a refreshing departure from Murphy's seemingly exclusive engagements of family-oriented comedies throughout the latter part of his career. Murphy is responsible for some of the biggest laughs in the film as he plays the criminal mentor to the amateur thieves. It's wonderful to be able to genuinely laugh at an Eddie Murphy performance again." (Brennan 2011) – *Dark Horizons*

On its opening domestic box office weekend of November 4-6, 2011, *Tower Heist* had a healthy debut in 2nd place. Below it in 3rd place was another new comedy release, *A Very Harold & Kumar Christmas* (2011), the final film in the *Harold & Kumar* trilogy after *Harold & Kumar Go to White Castle* (2004) and *Harold & Kumar Escape from Guantanamo Bay* (2008).

REVIEW

Heist movies are fun in theory because they consist of two parts: planning the heist and which team member is going to have which job, and then the execution of the heist itself. *Tower Heist* features a tip-top cast in a somewhat ludicrous heist that takes a bit of time to get going. A movie that's never as fun as it wants to be, *Tower Heist* is amiable enough but never rises to the occasion.

After billionaire Arthur Shaw (Alan Alda) embezzles the pension fund of employees at The Tower, his employees get their revenge by trying to get the hidden stash of $20 million he has in a safe in a room with heavy security. Leading the heist is Josh Kovaks (Ben Stiller), but there are plenty of others along for the ride wanting their piece of the action.

Matthew Broderick does well as the nebbish Wall Street investor who is part of the heist crew. Alan Alda is magnificent as the crafty billionaire ripping off everyone else. Eddie Murphy plays a supporting part, a rarity in his career, as Slide, a thief who uses his experiences to help the team. Less effective is the budding romance between Ben Stiller, the leader of the pack, and Téa Leoni, an FBI agent feeding them inside information.

So much time is spent setting up the heist that by the time it finally starts in earnest, the audience is too bored to care. The actual heist itself is pretty interesting involving a fair amount of suspense, but it starts way too late in the film. There's a good amount of sympathy built up to give good motivation as to why the heist is occurring, but a lot of the business around it (building up the team, planning out the heist, doing training runs) is often quite labored.

Eddie Murphy livens up the joint as Slide with jokes that hearken back to his earlier sexually-tinged material; both his flirtations with Gabourey Sidibe and his monologue on "lesbian titties" are quite memorable moments in a film that's amusing at best.

Featuring a retro horn-heavy 1970s score by Christophe Beck and a nice premise, *Tower Heist* is the kind of movie where the cast members are having more fun making it than the audience members are watching it. Brett Ratner gives the movie a nice scope, but it's in service to a heist that feels a bit run of the mill and lower in star wattage than the runaway success of Steven Soderbergh's modern *Ocean's Eleven* trilogy (*Ocean's Eleven, Ocean's Twelve,* and *Ocean's Thirteen*). An acceptable movie, *Tower Heist* never feels motivated enough to go the distance to stick out in a sea of heist pictures.

The Not-So Gems

Best Defense (1984)

(1984; Paramount Pictures) Director: Willard Huyck; Producer: Gloria Katz; Screenplay: Gloria Katz & Willard Huyck; Based on the Novel "Easy and Hard Ways Out" By: Robert Grossbach; Cinematographer: Donald Peterman; Editor: Sidney Wolinsky; Music: Patrick Williams; Cast: Kate Capshaw, George Dzundza, Dudley Moore, Christopher Maher, Eddie Murphy, Tom Noonan, David Rasche, Helen Shaver.

Unfortunately, they're both on our side.

THE MAKING OF BEST DEFENSE

- "[Paramount Pictures] told me, 'Eddie, we're not going to advertise much with you. It's a Dudley Moore film.' Next thing I know [on the posters and trailers], it's, 'Eddie Murphy! Back onscreen!' (Padilla n.d.) – Eddie Murphy (Actor)
- "It's a very funny action-comedy, but we never actually meet in it. We may have a scene together, but I doubt it. He's got some wonderfully funny stuff, so I'm looking forward to seeing him in it anyway." (T. B. Archive, Dudley Moore for "Unfaithfully Yours" 1984 - Bobbie Wygant Archive n.d.) – Dudley Moore (Actor)
- "Murphy never plays a meaningful role in the film's primary plot, nor does he interact with any other notable cast members. As detached from the narrative as he is, he is still Eddie Murphy, ultimately. While nothing he says or does comes close to the work he did before or would go on to do, he still effectively rescues *Best Defense* from being a completely miserable slog. I maybe laughed five times over the course of

94 minutes, and I'd wager that four of those were a result of Murphy's comic timing and delivery." (Pulaski 2023) – The Steve Pulaski Message Board

- "It's not that foreign policy and munitions aren't likely subjects for a real comedy, but Willard Huyck, who directed *Best Defense*, and Gloria Katz, who produced it, and who together wrote the screenplay, appear to have learned everything they ever wanted to know about the world by carefully reading weekly tabloids sold in supermarkets." (Canby 1984) – *The New York Times*

On its opening domestic box office weekend of July 20-22, 1984, *Best Defense* had a strong opening in 2nd place right below the reigning box office champ *Ghostbusters*. *Best Defense* opened higher than the other major new releases that weekend which included the cult-favorite fantasy film *The NeverEnding Story* (1984) and the geek-favorite comedy film *Revenge of the Nerds* (1984) (11th place).

REVIEW

An odd comedy based on the book "Easy and Hard Ways Out" by Richard Grossbach, *Best Defense* is a military contractor farce whose small Eddie Murphy presence confounds the film rather than elevates it. This is truly an Eddie Murphy movie in name only.

Wylie Cooper (Dudley Moore) is an engineer working on an experimental gyroscope for a tank for the military meant to enhance its targeting system. In the midst of his workplace stresses, Wylie's eyes wander from wife Laura (Kate Capshaw) to co-worker Clair (Helen Shaver). In a story set a few years in the future, Lieutenant T.M. Landy (Eddie Murphy) gets to try the gyroscope tank in Kuwait in combat to mixed results.

Part of the reason the two stories never work when intercut with each other is that their tone is so different. Moore's story, the meat of the movie, is a comedy of manners featuring a more verbal British style of humor rife with KGB spycraft and farcical characters. Murphy's story is more of an American comedy focusing on explosions and more explicit sex jokes delivered in a more laconic manner. In other words, viewers aren't getting more bang for their buck here. Instead, just as they are comprehending what is happening in one part of the story, the movie lurches to the wholly unrelated other part. It's a jostling transition every time.

The Dudley Moore (*Arthur* (1981), *Santa Claus: The Movie* (1985)) sequences work a good bit better. Dudley Moore is quite good when flirting with Helen Shaver (*In Praise of Older Women* (1978), *The Color of Money* (1986)) or joking around with George Dzundza (*No Mercy* (1986), *The Deer Hunter* (1978)). Had this been a simple office comedy set around the complications of a workplace affair, things would have gone a bit more swimmingly. Instead, the military and spy components complicate the story and humor to such a degree (repeating "The WAM's overheating!" line over and over again doesn't make it any funnier, folks) that anything enjoyable gets lost in the bureaucratic shuffle.

Eddie Murphy's story answers the not so lingering question whether Dudley's Moore new targeting system works in the field, but it would have been more fun to integrate Murphy and Moore into the same story somehow. Production photos exist of a scene filmed with both actors, but the scene itself was cut from the final movie. How bad could it have been?

Best Defense combines military and office farces into an over-baked and overblown comedy that is a real drag. Both Dudley Moore and Eddie Murphy, comedy legends in their own right, are a complete and total waste here.

I Spy (2002)

(2002; Sony Pictures Releasing) Director: Betty Thomas; Producers: Mario Kassar, Betty Thomas, Jenno Topping, Andrew G. Vajna; Screenplay: Marianne Wibberley & Cormac Wibberley, Jay Scherick & David Ronn; Story: Marianne Wibberley & Cormac Wibberley; Based on Characters Created By: Morton S. Fine & David Friedkin; Cinematographer: Oliver Wood; Editor: Peter Teschner; Music: Richard Gibbs; Cast: Lynda Boyd, Gary Cole, Famke Janssen, Sugar Ray Leonard, Phill Lewis, Eddie Murphy, Malcolm McDowell, Owen Wilson.

Attitude meets espionage.

THE MAKING OF I SPY

- "Maybe 70% of what you see is in the script and then we improvised. We liked to make stuff up and have fun. Some of my best stuff is stuff we just came up with on the set. In a movie like this, the relationship between the two guys is crucial. It sinks or swims on how these two guys are together. I think we did a good job." (Cawthorne n.d.) – Eddie Murphy (Actor)
- "They originally wrote this [part as a] tennis player, basketball player. And Eddie says, 'I don't know how to do any of these things, if can't do of those. I don't know how to play basketball, I'm the worst. If you have to do anything, could you do boxing? That would really turn me on.'" (Anthony n.d.) – Betty Thomas (Director)
- "We tried to have props that in some way told you a little bit more about each character. For example, Owen's character feels like he always gets the really crappy equipment." (BluRay n.d.) – Jenno Topping (Producer)

- "There are a few funny moments involving Robinson's henchmen, and the scene in which Wilson sings Marvin Gaye's "Sexual Healing" is definitely worth a chuckle, but that's about it." (Levinson 2015) – *The Oberlin Review*
- "If there is any saving grace to be found in *I Spy*, it's that the stunts are fairly well done, the comedy is predictable but steady, and the one-liners are mercifully not complete groaners." (Horn 2002) – IGN

On its opening domestic box office weekend of November 1-3, 2002, *I Spy* opened in 3rd place (Box Office Mojo n.d.). It was beat out by the other major new release that week, the Tim Allen Christmas comedy sequel *The Santa Clause 2* (2002).

REVIEW

The late 1990s and early 2000s were a big time for spy spoofs (*Austin Powers: International Man of Mystery* (1997), *Johnny English* (2003)) and feature-film reboots of TV shows (*A Very Brady Sequel* (1996), *Sgt. Bilko* (1996)). While *I Spy* has the makings for a fun team-up (Eddie Murphy's fast wisecracks plus Owen Wilson's slacker patois just can't miss!), Betty Thomas' lackluster approach to the material makes this one of Eddie Murphy's worst.

Special Agent Alex Scott (Owen Wilson) is set on preventing the dastardly Arnold Gundars (Malcolm McDowell) from selling a stealth fighter prototype to the highest bidder. For overly complicated plot reasons, boxing king Kelly Robinson (Eddie Murphy) is brought in to be an undercover spy alongside Alex Scott. Explosions and zaniness ensue.

Eddie Murphy isn't the problem here. He plays Kelly Robinson as a very excitable sports superstar. Murphy is in top physical shape here, giving a hyper line delivery that brings to mind the signature delivery of Don King. Kelly Robinson is a man used to glitz and glamor, and it's fun to see him freak out during the action scenes.

On the other hand, Owen Wilson (*Anaconda* (1997), *How Do You Know* (2010)) is kind of on autopilot here. There's a give and take between him and Agent Carlos (a memorably hammy Gary Cole) that has a spark or two, but the character is too much like Wilson's normal whiny persona to stick out from the crowd. He had more chemistry with Jackie Chan in *Shanghai Noon* (2000) than he does with Eddie Murphy here!

Malcolm McDowell (*Schweitzer* (1990), *Star Trek: Generations* (1994)) cruises through the movie as a villain who's barely onscreen. He flashes his evil grin and laughs like he's done in so many generic thrillers that it's a wonder they didn't cast someone else. It would have been fun for McDowell to get some juicy scenes to play off Murphy and Wilson, but that doesn't happen here.

Whether it's the wonky effects of the stealth plane or the endless action scenes near the end, there's a lifelessness to just about every scene in *I Spy*. Other than Famke Janssen (*Lord of Illusions* (1995), *Taken 2* (2012)) giving her role some zest as a confident, sexy tongue-in-cheek special agent, there's really nothing to see here. Couldn't they have given Bill Cosby a cameo?

Eddie Murphy in a spy comedy should have been a no-brainer. It'd be fun to see Eddie Murphy do a serious spy movie that plays to his strengths instead of this wobbly comedy. Awful in its utter mediocrity, *I Spy* is one to skip.

Meet Dave (2002)

(2002; Twentieth Century Fox) Director: Brian Robbins; Producers: Jon Berg, David T. Friendly, Todd Komarnicki; Screenplay: Rob Greenberg & Bill Corbett; Cinematographer: Clark Mathis; Editor: Ned Bastille; Cast: Elizabeth Banks, Scott Caan, Judah Friedlander, Kevin Hart, Ed Helms, Austyn Myers, Eddie Murphy, Gabrielle Union.

Eddie Murphy in Eddie Murphy.

THE MAKING OF MEET DAVE

- "Well, to be honest, [*Meet Dave*] came about when I was finishing up *Norbit* with Eddie and he had already been involved in developing it, and he gave it to me. When I read it, I thought, 'Wow. This is a kind of cool premise.' It's something we hadn't seen before and I thought the opportunity for him to sort of play this sort of robot, so to speak, was a cool thing for him to do, and lent itself to some really great comedic situations." – Brian Robbins (Director)
- "I knew we would face problems getting the cameras into positions on our New York City background plates that would allow us to shoot all the angles that our director Brian Robbins and our Director of Photography Clark Mathis wanted to use when shooting Eddie Murphy and Gabrielle Union. Brian's and Clark's challenge to me was to let them shoot Eddie as if he was a normal-sized actor, including normal, slightly low angles up to their faces for their medium shots and their close-ups. This meant the plate camera would be half-buried in the street in Times Square to get the lens low enough to find the technically correct matching

angle. In Times Square, this was not an option." (Wolff 2008) – Mark Stetson (Visual Effects Supervisor)

- "I was doing my best to sell screenplays. I eventually sold one: *Meet Dave*, with Eddie Murphy. It turned out to be kind of a shitty movie, but it was a really interesting experience, because I saw how bad movies can be made. I actually liked a lot of the people I was working with—they were not stereotypically creepy Hollywood producers. But when you are creating something so huge—and something that involves so many people with high stakes, often working at cross purposes—the odds of any movie being genuinely good are pretty low." (Raftery 2014) – Bill Corbett (Screenwriter)

- "It also gets rather annoying that after almost every single one of Dave's awkward encounters Murphy feels the need to mug in front of the camera, which makes it seem like he's trying to remind us that what we are seeing is supposed to be funny. (It also doesn't help that some of the jokes are just blatant advertisements for such businesses as Old Navy, Apple, Google, Yahoo and MySpace.)" (Tobias 2008) – *The Watertown Daily Times*

- "Maybe [*Meet Dave* is] a little more ambitious than some of his more recent stuff and it's certainly less blatantly evil than *Norbit*, but that doesn't matter. As a human being you know instinctively whether or not you're the right audience for it. If you are, buy a ticket and then hate yourself in the morning. I understand. I'm not going to judge you for it. At least he's not Chevy Chase." (Tyler 2016) – *Cinema Blend*

On its opening domestic box office on July 11-13, 2008, *Meet Dave* opened in 7th place (Box Office Mojo n.d.). The other major new releases of the weekend included the comic book movie *Hellboy II: The Golden Army* and the family film *Journey to the Center of the Earth* (2008), which opened in 1ˢᵗ and 3ʳᵈ place, respectively.

REVIEW

A good comedy is hard to find; when you combine comedy with science fiction, it's even harder. *Meet Dave* valiantly attempts to straddle the line between goofy antics aimed at kids and a lot of jokes where characters are behind control panels. If nothing else, *Meet Dave* has ambitions thanks to its trippy premise.

A humanoid spaceship crashes onto Earth. Naming itself somewhat improbably as Dave Ming Chang (Eddie Murphy), it's piloted by a crew of humanoid aliens named by number including, but not limited to, Number 1 (Eddie Murphy speaking in a British accent), Number 2 (Ed Helms), Number 3 (Gabrielle Union), and Number 17 (Kevin Hart). In short order, Dave meets Gina (Elizabeth Banks), a single mom who is raising her son Josh (Austyn Myers). Zaniness ensues.

Meet Dave has far too complicated a plot for a studio comedy aimed at tots. Once things get going after the convoluted premise finds its footing (does the humanoid spaceship really need dozens of tiny aliens commanding it?), *Meet Dave* starts to have moments of fun. Eddie Murphy is at his best here trying to act human as the humanoid spaceship Dave in a well-meaning, but stilted, manner. What doesn't work, and what the movie seems to think is far more amusing, is all the crew antics taking place inside of Dave. Among other things, we see a coup, blossoming romances, and crying while watching movies. Just because a scene is zany doesn't mean it drives the story forward or that it's funny in the first place. To be blunt, *Meet Dave* doesn't hold a candle to the conceptually similar *Innerspace* (1987).

Eddie Murphy has some good rapport with being a sort of protective father figure to the cherubic Austyn Myers. Scott Caan (*Ready to Rumble* (2000), *Sonny* (2002)) is decent as a cop on the trail of Eddie Murphy's weird antics around New York City. A young Kevin Hart (*Soul Plane* (2004), *Think Like a Man Too* (2014)) throws himself into some physical comedy with gusto as Number 17, especially when he gets to act drunk. Elizabeth Banks (*Our Idiot Brother* (2011), *Spider-Man 3* (2007)) is kind of wasted here as a mom who does little else except to be super nice all the time.

Meet Dave has a clever concept but is a tepid motion picture at best. Easily one of Eddie Murphy's worst, *Meet Dave* is a turgid waste of a fun premise.

Vampire in Brooklyn (1995)

(1995; Paramount Pictures) Director: Wes Craven; Producers: Mark Lipsky, Eddie Murphy; Screenplay: Charlie Murphy, Michael Lucker & Chris Parker; Story: Eddie Murphy & Vernon Lynch, Eddie Murphy; Cinematographer: Mark Irwin; Editor: Patrick Lussier; Cast: Angela Bassett, Joanna Cassidy, Kadeem Hardison, Simbi Kali, Eddie Murphy, Allen Payne, Mitch Pileggi, John Witherspoon.

A comic tale of horror and seduction.

THE MAKING OF VAMPIRE IN BROOKLYN

- "I remember the first time I was really frightened by a picture, and that was *The Exorcist*. I was baptized Catholic, had a Catholic upbringing, all this stuff... It horrified me, you know. When the commercials for it came on TV, you'd hear the music, and I'd run to turn the sound down so I wouldn't hear it." (Leydon n.d.) – Eddie Murphy (Actor/ Writer/Producer)
- "Horror is very close to humor. The thing is I wanted the humor in *Vampire in Brooklyn* to come from the story – from the plot, not from Eddie. I wanted Eddie to be essentially a serious character. What I didn't want was just a black version of *Love at First Bite*. I didn't think *Love at First Bite* was very funny. I didn't want the comedy to be nearly that broad." (Vincent 1995) – Wes Craven (Director)
- "But the worst thing about ad-libbing is that when you shoot it again, you don't remember what you said. So [Wes Craven] would take notes and tell me what I said. I said, 'I said that?' So many lines that you say you forget that you say anything— you're just ad-libbing, you're not committing it to memory. So it was kind of difficult working with him, because he shot

a lot of scenes, you know, instead of shooting one scene and get the genius of it all, he'd shoot it from different angles." (Rabin, Random Roles: John Witherspoon 2012) – John Witherspoon (Actor)

- "Though there's a joke about the blaxploitation pic *Blacula*, in tone and execution [*Vampire in Brooklyn*] more closely recalls the 1985 movie *Fright Night* in presenting Murphy as Maximillian — a suave, earthy vampire galivanting around New York." (Lowry 1995) – *Variety*
- "To be fair, Eddie Murphy does a better-than-average job as Maximillian, the last vampire on Earth. There are moments when Murphy is positively chilling, and he doesn't ham it up too much. Comedy is mixed in effectively, but it's what the humor is mingled with that doesn't work. As a horror film, *Vampire in Brooklyn* is a failure." (Berardinelli n.d.) – *ReelViews*

On its opening weekend of October 27-29, 1995, *Vampire in Brooklyn* opened in 3rd place in the domestic box office (Box Office Mojo n.d.). Other major new flicks opening that weekend were the Jeff Goldblum science-fiction drama *Powder* (1995) in 2nd place, the Sigourney Weaver serial killer procedural *Copycat* (1995) in 4th place, and the Patrick Swayze family film *Three Wishes* (1995). Adding to the crowded weekend were two big Oscar contenders opening in limited release, Woody Allen's romantic comedy *Mighty Aphrodite* (1995) and Nicolas Cage's alcoholism drama *Leaving Las Vegas* (1995).

REVIEW

Wes Craven and Eddie Murphy working together should have made an interesting film. Horror and comedy are a combo that can work well because both genres rely on surprise through suspense. It's quite a pity, then, that *Vampire in Brooklyn* lurches around for its entire running time failing to find much of an effective footing. There are funny scenes and there are violent scenes, but nothing's cohesive here. The entire movie is like a fledgling vampire sucking more blood in one go than it should, gagging on its own supply.

In Brooklyn, the vampire Maximillian (Eddie Murphy) battles gangsters while falling in love with Detective Rita Veder (Angela Bassett). As Veder comes to terms with her own half-vampire origins, she has to decide whether to embrace or reject Maximillian.

Mark Irwin's cinematography (*American Pie 2* (2001), *Scream* (1996)) gives the movie a slick shadowy look, emphasizing the horror vibes. *Vampire in Brooklyn* fails to embrace either the horror or the comedy, making both feel out of place. To make things worse, Eddie Murphy and Angela Bassett (*Critters 4* (1992), *Jumping the Broom* (2011)) have some real heat that's wasted here. Viewers are jerked from scene to scene like they are riding Big Thunder Mountain Railroad at Disney Land.

Eddie's typical move of playing multiple characters doesn't work as well here as it does in *Norbit* or *The Nutty Professor*. The main character of Maximillian has a Jamaican accent that sort of works, and Eddie is good at making him scary when the script calls for it. The real problem is, the other two characters Murphy plays are so damn broad it feels like you're watching a lesser *Looney Tunes* short. Preacher Pauly is a Southern preacher that, while funny, we've seen a million times before. Worse is the gangster Guido whose scenes are more annoying than anything else.

Vampire in Brooklyn is a rather sluggish attempt for Eddie Murphy to try something new. It can be fun seeing him play a bad guy, but a cluttered screenplay with an uneven mix of genres sinks this motion picture. A lackadaisical film, *Vampire in Brooklyn* would have been better off buried.

Afterword

After successfully pitching a book on *The Films of Eddie Murphy* to BearManor Media, I came in with some assumptions. I figured I had seen most of the Eddie Murphy movies. I also thought that I would find Eddie Murphy's decades-long shift into more family-friendly material a waste of his considerable comedic talents. I was wrong on both counts.

Looking at Eddie's entire filmography, it became clear I had really only seen half of his films. I was going to rewatch all the movies for the book anyway, but watching a movie that's new to me is always a harder task than watching a film I had seen before. It also makes writing a book fresher because a lot of the subject is new to me, and, for all I know, new to the reader as well.

Rewatching Eddie's *oeuvre*, it became clear that his work was often just as good in his family films as his edgy comedies. Even if some of these films could be a bit of a mixed bag to put it kindly, Murphy always tried something different in them whether it's being mostly silent in *A Thousand Words* or playing a role where he has no jokes other than a mild gag about Apple Jacks cereal in *Mr. Church*.

In more recent years, it's been fascinating watching Eddie Murphy come full circle doing what some call legacy sequels to his hit films. In the past four years, he's made a second *Coming to America* film and a fourth *Beverly Hills Cop*. A third *48 Hrs.* is rumored to be in the works.

In a June 29, 2024, interview with David Marchese for *The New York Times*, Eddie Murphy reflected on the quality of the films throughout his career: "I have more than five good [movies], though. I feel like I have maybe five or six bad ones. You know, "Pluto Nash" might be the only [expletive] movie. I have a couple of movies that are soft, and movies that are just OK. But no flops." (Marchese 2024).

I may disagree with Eddie Murphy's ratings of his own films (what I wouldn't give to see his rankings from best to worst!), but, in the end, I think watching his whole filmography is a journey worth taking. During the period in which this book was written (December 2023 through November 2024), all of his movies except for one were available to rent or purchase digitally through different streaming platforms in the United States.

The sole film only available on disc is what I find to be one of the better films in Eddie Murphy's filmography, *The Distinguished Gentleman*. No streaming service had it available for rental or purchase; I had to buy a non-anamorphic DVD to watch it. Good thing my Sony PlayStation 5 doubles as a DVD player! *The Distinguished Gentleman* deserves a re-release on modern 4K Blu-ray and digital formats at some point in the not-too-distant future. It deserves to be seen on its own merits as a comedy and would be an entertaining way to introduce students to political satire to boot.

If you'll forgive me, I'll wrap up this afterword with an anecdote when I visited the local Media Play, a DVD retail store in the early 2000s. I asked the store clerk, who looked six years younger than me, "Where do you have your Eddie Murphy movies?" He paused and pointed to an aisle in the back. "You'll want to check out our Family films!" I frowned. "Don't you mean the Comedy section?" I replied. The clerk shook his head, correcting me: "Oh no, Eddie Murphy doesn't make any comedies. He just makes family films!" I wept for future generations.

Mat Bradley-Tschirgi, November 19, 2024

Bibliography

Adams, Derek. 2014. *Mulan.* April 23. Accessed October 27, 2024. https://www.timeout.com/movies/mulan-1.

Addicted to TV. n.d. *Karey Kirkpatrick interview for Imagine That.* Accessed November 15, 2024. https://www.youtube.com/watch?v=TKZqm0xaYjI.

Addiego, Walter. 1998. *The animals get all the good lines.* June 26. Accessed October 25, 2024. https://www.sfgate.com/news/article/the-animals-get-all-the-good-lines-3082636.php.

All-Access Universal Pictures. n.d. *Eddie Murphy Behind the Voice of Donkey | Shrek.* Accessed October 30, 2024. https://www.youtube.com/watch?v=4XbfCRomRRM.

AllTrailersMov. n.d. *Shrek the Third Justin Timberlake 2007.* Accessed October 31, 2024. https://www.youtube.com/watch?v=Bxo-oEr8npY.

American Cinematographer. 2006. *Woody Omens, ASC.* January. Accessed November 14, 2024. https://theasc.com/magazine/jan06/omens/page2.html.

American Masters PBS. n.d. *Herbie Hancock on jazz and Quincy Jones' influence | American Masters | PBS.* Accessed November 14, 2024. https://www.youtube.com/watch?v=Wlk373ylcTE.

Andersen, Soren. 2016. *'Mr. Church' cooks up a tear-jerker with Eddie Murphy.* September 15. Accessed November 4, 2024. https://www.seattletimes.com/entertainment/movies/mr-church-cooks-up-a-tear-jerker-with-eddie-murphy/?utm_source=RSS&utm_medium=Referral&utm_campaign=RSS_movies.

Andrew, Geoff. 2012. *Eddie Murphy Raw.* September 10. Accessed November 3, 2024. https://www.timeout.com/movies/eddie-murphy-raw-1.

Ansen, David. 2007. *No More Mickey Mouse: Animation for Adults.* May 20. Accessed October 31, 2024. https://www.newsweek.com/no-more-mickey-mouse-animation-adults-100981.

—. 2000. *Thin Story About A Fat Man.* 8 6. Accessed 10 29, 2024. https://www.newsweek.com/thin-story-about-fat-man-158923.

Anthony, Ross. n.d. *I Spy Interviews.* Accessed November 18, 2024. https://www.rossanthony.com/interviews/ispyint.shtml.

Arar, Yardena. 1983. *Performers sparkle in Trading Places.* June 25. Accessed November 4, 2024. https://cdnc.ucr.edu/cgi-bin/cdnc?a=d&d=DS19830625.2.160&e=-------en--20--1--txt-txIN--------.

Armstrong, Josh. 2007. *Directors Miller and Hui on Shrek the Third.* May 21. Accessed October 31, 2024. https://animatedviews.com/2007/miller-hui-on-shrek-3/.

Arrose, Koko. n.d. *Jurgen Prochnow Q&A BIFFF 2008.* Accessed October 13, 2024. https://www.youtube.com/watch?v=5wZ8HlzPxMI.

Attanasio, Paul. 1986. *Golden Child: Murphy's Law.* December 12. Accessed November 3, 2024. https://www.washingtonpost.com/archive/lifestyle/1986/12/12/golden-child-murphys-law/30fcce53-614a-4fb2-bfdc-68af8814c7e1/.

Audio, Spitfire. n.d. *Jermaine Stegall composed whilst on set for Coming 2 America.* Accessed October 21, 2024. https://composer.spitfireaudio.com/en/articles/jermaine-stegall-composed-whilst-on-set-for-coming-2-america.

Baumgarten, Marjorie. 1992. *Boomerang.* July 3. Accessed November 2, 2024. https://www.austinchronicle.com/events/film/1992-07-03/boomerang/.

—. 1999. *Life.* April 16. Accessed November 3, 2024. https://www.austinchronicle.com/events/film/1999-04-16/142881/.

Bell, BreAnna. 2023. *Netflix Top 10: 'You People' Debuts at No. 1 for English-Language Movies With More Than 55 Million Hours*

Watched. January 31. Accessed November 4, 2024. https://variety.com/2023/tv/news/you-people-netflix-55-million-hours-viewed-opening-weekend-1235508210/.

Berardinelli, James. n.d. *Vampire in Brooklyn (United States, 1995).* Accessed November 19, 2024. https://www.reelviews.net/reelviews/vampire-in-brooklyn.

Bergren, Joe. 2018. *'Mulan' Turns 20: Ming-Na Wen Reflects on Animated Disney Classic (Exclusive).* June 19. Accessed October 27, 2024. https://www.yahoo.com/entertainment/mulan-turns-20-ming-na-140857820.html.

Berkman, Meredith. 1992. *Eddie Murphy in 'Boomerang'.* July 10. Accessed November 2, 2024. https://ew.com/article/1992/07/10/eddie-murphy-boomerang/.

—. 1992. *Eddie Murphy's second coming.* December 18. Accessed November 2, 2024. https://ew.com/article/1992/12/18/eddie-murphys-second-coming/.

BFI. n.d. *In conversation with... John Landis and Deborah Nadoolman Landis on Coming to America | BFI.* Accessed October 20, 2024. https://www.youtube.com/watch?v=BeJH1EG91Pk.

BlackTree TV. n.d. *Imagine That Premiere w/ K. Kirkpatrick and Vanessa Williams.* Accessed November 15, 2024. https://www.youtube.com/watch?v=AmStuIyxv_o.

Blackwelder, Rob. n.d. *Metro.* Accessed November 15, 2024. https://splicedwire.com/97reviews/metro.html.

Bland, Simon. 2023. *Trading Places director John Landis says 'offensive' moments require perspective.* December 14. Accessed November 4, 2024. https://uk.movies.yahoo.com/movies/trading-places-director-john-landis-offensive-moments-150956114.html.

Blay, Zeba. 2023. *'You People' and the Tediousness of the Interracial Romcom.* January 26. Accessed November 4, 2024. https://www.jezebel.com/you-people-and-the-tediousness-of-the-interracial-romco-1850037153.

Borrelli, Christopher. 2003. *Movie review: Daddy Day Care **.* May 9. Accessed November 6, 2024. https://www.toledoblade.com/Movies/2003/05/09/Movie-review-Daddy-Day-Care.html.

Box Office Mojo . n.d. *Domestic 1987 Weekend 51.* Accessed November 3, 2024. https://www.boxofficemojo.com/weekend/1987W51/?ref_=bo_rl_table_1.

—. n.d. *Domestic 2012 Weekend 10.* Accessed November 6, 2024. https://www.boxofficemojo.com/weekend/2012W10/?ref_=bo_rl_table_1.

Box Office Mojo. n.d. *Domestic 1982 Weekend 50.* Accessed October 7, 2024. https://www.boxofficemojo.com/weekend/1982W50/?ref_=bo_rl_table_1.

—. n.d. *Domestic 1984 Weekend 49.* Accessed October 11, 2024. https://www.boxofficemojo.com/weekend/1984W49/?ref_=bo_rl_table_1.

—. n.d. *Domestic 1987 Weekend 21.* Accessed October 13, 2024. https://www.boxofficemojo.com/weekend/1987W21/?ref_=bo_rl_table_1.

—. n.d. *Domestic 1989 Weekend 46.* Accessed November 15, 2024. https://www.boxofficemojo.com/weekend/1989W46/?ref_=bo_rl_table_1.

—. n.d. *Domestic 1990 Weekend 23.* Accessed October 9, 2024. https://www.boxofficemojo.com/weekend/1990W23/?ref_=bo_rl_table_1.

—. n.d. *Domestic 1992 Weekend 49.* Accessed November 2, 2024. https://www.boxofficemojo.com/weekend/1992W49/?ref_=bo_rl_table_1.

—. n.d. *Domestic 1994 Weekend 21.* Accessed October 13, 2024. https://www.boxofficemojo.com/weekend/1994W21/occasion/us_memorialday_weekend/?ref_=bo_rl_table_2.

—. n.d. *Domestic 1995 Weekend 43.* Accessed November 19, 2024. https://www.boxofficemojo.com/weekend/1995W43/?ref_=bo_rl_table_1.

—. n.d. *Domestic 1996 Weekend 26*. Accessed October 27, 2004. https://www.boxofficemojo.com/weekend/1996W26/?ref_=bo_rl_table_1.

—. n.d. *Domestic 1998 Weekend 25*. Accessed October 27, 2024. https://www.boxofficemojo.com/weekend/1998W25/?ref_=bo_rl_table_1.

—. n.d. *Domestic 1998 Weekend 26*. Accessed October 25, 2024. https://www.boxofficemojo.com/weekend/1998W26/?ref_=bo_rl_table_1.

—. n.d. *Domestic 1998 Weekend 41*. Accessed November 15, 2024. https://www.boxofficemojo.com/weekend/1998W41/?ref_=bo_rl_table_1.

—. n.d. *Domestic 1999 Weekend 16*. Accessed November 3, 2024. https://www.boxofficemojo.com/weekend/1999W16/?ref_=bo_rl_table_1.

—. n.d. *Domestic 1999 Weekend 33*. Accessed November 2, 2024. https://www.boxofficemojo.com/weekend/1999W33/?ref_=bo_rl_table_1.

—. n.d. *Domestic 2000 Weekend 30*. Accessed 10 29, 2024. https://www.boxofficemojo.com/weekend/2000W30/?ref_=bo_rl_table_1.

—. n.d. *Domestic 2001 Weekend 20*. Accessed 10 30, 2024. https://www.boxofficemojo.com/weekend/2001W20/?ref_=bo_rl_table_1.

—. n.d. *Domestic 2001 Weekend 25*. Accessed October 25, 2024. https://www.boxofficemojo.com/weekend/2001W25/?ref_=bo_rl_table_1.

—. n.d. *Domestic 2002 Weekend 11*. Accessed November 17, 2024. https://www.boxofficemojo.com/weekend/2002W11/?ref_=bo_rl_table_1.

—. n.d. *Domestic 2002 Weekend 33*. Accessed November 17, 2024. https://www.boxofficemojo.com/weekend/2002W33/?ref_=bo_rl_table_1.

—. n.d. *Domestic 2002 Weekend 44.* Accessed November 18, 2024. https://www.boxofficemojo.com/weekend/2002W44/?ref_=bo_rl_table_1.

—. n.d. *Domestic 2006 Weekend 50.* Accessed November 3, 2024. https://www.boxofficemojo.com/weekend/2006W50/?ref_=bo_rl_table_1.

—. n.d. *Domestic 2007 Weekend 20.* Accessed October 31, 2024. https://www.boxofficemojo.com/weekend/2007W20/?ref_=bo_rl_table_1.

—. n.d. *Domestic 2007 Weekend 6.* Accessed November 17, 2024. https://www.boxofficemojo.com/weekend/2007W06/?ref_=bo_rl_table_1.

—. n.d. *Domestic 2008 Weekend 28.* Accessed November 18, 2024. https://www.boxofficemojo.com/weekend/2008W28/?ref_=bo_rl_table_1.

—. n.d. *Domestic 2016 Weekend 38.* Accessed November 4, 2024. https://www.boxofficemojo.com/weekend/2016W38/?ref_=bo_rl_table_1.

Brennan, Tom. 2011. *Review: Tower Heist.* November 5. Accessed November 17, 2024. https://www.darkhorizons.com/review-tower-heist/.

Breznican, Anthony. n.d. *'Bowfinger' director likes light, dark.* Accessed November 2, 2024. https://eu.southcoasttoday.com/story/entertainment/local/1999/08/14/bowfinger-director-likes-light/50512807007/.

British Cinematographer. n.d. *Sex Bomb.* Accessed November 17, 2024. https://britishcinematographer.co.uk/thomas-kloss-don-jon/.

—. n.d. *Towering Achievements.* Accessed November 17, 2024. https://britishcinematographer.co.uk/dante-spinotti-special-feature/.

Brooks, Melanie, and Anthony D'Alessandro. 2024. *Judge Reinhold On Being Cast In Original 'Beverly Hills Cop' Before Eddie Murphy Signed On – 'Axel F' Premiere.* June 24. Accessed

October 11, 2024. https://deadline.com/2024/06/beverly-hills-cop-axel-f-judge-reinhold-sylvester-stallone-1235982364/.

Bynes, Paul. 2010. *Shrek Forever After.* June 10. Accessed November 2, 2024. https://www.smh.com.au/entertainment/movies/shrek-forever-after-20100609-xwjw.html.

Byrge, Duane. n.d. *'Coming to America': THR's 1988 Review.* Accessed October 20, 2024. https://www.hollywoodreporter.com/movies/movie-news/coming-america-review-1988-movie-1017600/.

Campione, Katie. 2023. *'Candy Cane Lane': Amazon Boasts Sweet Premiere Weekend For Eddie Murphy Holiday Comedy.* December 6. Accessed November 2, 2024. https://deadline.com/2023/12/candy-cane-lane-ratings-amazon-1235654326/.

Canby, Vincent. 1984. *A Comedy About Munitions.* July 20. Accessed November 17, 2024. https://www.nytimes.com/1984/07/20/movies/a-comedy-about-munitions.html.

Carter, Jimmy. n.d. *Eddie Murphy interview "Metro" 1997.* Accessed November 15, 2024. https://www.youtube.com/watch?v=a-HgTHHP55c.

Cawthorne, Alec. n.d. *BBC Films Interview Eddie Murphy I Spy.* Accessed November 18, 2024. https://www.bbc.co.uk/films/2003/01/10/eddie_murphy_i_spy_interview.shtml.

CELEBS.com. n.d. *Eddie Murphy's Official Shrek the Final Chapter Interview - Celebs.com.* Accessed October 24, 2024. https://www.youtube.com/watch?v=NUJJ34oJIKQ.

Červinka, Petr. n.d. *The Making of Mulan.* Accessed October 27, 2024. https://www.youtube.com/watch?v=-zHSJBwhuUk.

Chang, Justin. 2012. *A Thousand Words.* March 8. Accessed November 6, 2024. https://variety.com/2012/film/reviews/a-thousand-words-1117947208/.

Cinema.com. n.d. *Dr Dolittle 2 : Production Notes.* Accessed October 25, 2024. https://www.cinema.com/articles/453/dr-dolittle-2-production-notes.phtml.

Clarke, Donald. 2024. *Beverly Hills Cop: Axel F review – Eddie Murphy's comic gifts still in place but this looks to have staggered in from another century.* July 3. Accessed October 20, 2024. https://www.irishtimes.com/culture/film/review/2024/07/03/beverly-hills-cop-axel-f-review-eddie-murphys-comic-gifts-still-in-place-but-this-looks-to-have-staggered-in-from-another-century/.

Clement, Nick. 2020. *The Billy Weber Interview: Part Two.* June 3. Accessed October 13, 2024. https://wearecult.rocks/the-billy-weber-interview-part-two.

Click on Detroit | Local 4 | WDIV. n.d. *Remembering the life of Gil Hill.* Accessed October 11, 2024. https://www.youtube.com/watch?v=R7IPMLzA2JE.

CNN Larry King Live. 2002. *Interview with William Shatner.* February 21. Accessed November 17, 2024. https://transcripts.cnn.com/show/lkl/date/2002-02-21/segment/00.

Comics, Beer & Sci-fi. n.d. *Actor Ronny Cox | Comics, Beer and Sci-fi.* Accessed October 11, 2024. https://www.youtube.com/watch?v=deyXEIo8BI4.

Compton, Michael. 2012. *'A Thousand Words' is unspeakably bad.* March 12. Accessed November 6, 2024. https://www.bgdailynews.com/community/a-thousand-words-is-unspeakably-bad/article_6e7d02c6-6c7e-11e1-a9ba-001871e3ce6c.html.

D'Alessandro, Anthony. 2007. *Tobias A. Schliessler, 'Dreamgirls'.* January 3. Accessed November 3, 2024. https://variety.com/2007/film/awards/tobias-a-schliessler-dreamgirls-1117956610/.

Daniel Fee33. n.d. *Martin Brest FIRST VIDEO INTERVIEW in 25 YEARS! Oscar-Nominated Director!* Accessed October 11, 2024. https://www.youtube.com/watch?v=1UcFux2wqH0.

Davis, Steve. 2007. *Norbit.* February 9. Accessed November 17, 2024. https://www.austinchronicle.com/events/film/2007-02-09/443314/.

Dick, Jeremy. 2024. *'I Forced Myself to Stop': Eddie Murphy Recalls Retiring Trademark Laugh.* June 27. Accessed October 11, 2024. https://www.cbr.com/eddie-murphy-trademark-laugh/.

Director's Guild of America. n.d. *Michael Ritchie Chapter 4.* Accessed November 3, 2024. https://www.dga.org/VideoHTMLNew.ashx?id=%7BECCEC845-8AA1-466E-8D44-656CDE309E55%7D&db=web.

Dursin, Andre. n.d. *Aisle SEAT Special: The JOHN LANDIS Interview.* Accessed October 20, 2024. https://www.andyfilm.com/landis.html.

DVDXtras. n.d. *The Haunted Mansion (2003) | Behind the Scenes + Deleted Scenes.* Accessed October 26, 2024. https://www.youtube.com/watch?v=2mSx-_awLxI.

E! Insider. n.d. *"Shrek" Turns 20: Live From E! Rewind | E! Red Carpet & Award Shows.* Accessed 10 30, 2024. https://www.youtube.com/watch?v=ezJ59lQ_xBk.

Eat_Your_Make-Up. n.d. *Dr Dolittle 2: Making Movie Magic with Rhythm and Hues VHS RIP.* Accessed October 25, 2024. https://www.youtube.com/watch?v=MS-unBq0zXs.

Ebert, Roger. 1989. *Harlem Nights.* November 17. Accessed November 14, 2024. https://www.rogerebert.com/reviews/harlem-nights-1989.

—. 1986. *The Golden Child.* December 12. Accessed November 3, 2024. https://www.rogerebert.com/reviews/the-golden-child-1986.

—. 1996. *The Nutty Professor.* June 28. Accessed October 27, 2024. https://www.rogerebert.com/reviews/the-nutty-professor-1996.

Eddie Murphy Comedy. n.d. *Eddie Murphy - Trading Places Interview: Cast & Director.* Accessed November 4, 2024. https://www.youtube.com/watch?v=Y90_4oxEoFU.

—. n.d. *Eddie Murphy Funny Interview On The Making of 48 Hours.* Accessed October 7, 2024. https://www.youtube.com/watch?v=4ToqTN7UfRU.

Edrive. 1998. *Edrive.com Chat with Jeff Goldblum.* October 7. Accessed November 15, 2024. https://www.goldblum.com/interviews/interview13.html.

Ellis, Kirk. 1984. *'Beverly Hills Cop': THR's 1984 Review.* December 5. Accessed October 11, 2024. https://www.hollywoodreporter.com/news/general-news/beverly-hills-cop-1984-review-952752/.

Empire Online. 2000. *The Haunted Mansion Review.* January 1. Accessed October 26, 2024. https://www.empireonline.com/movies/reviews/haunted-mansion-2-review/.

Erbland, Kate. 2024. *The One Thing 'Beverly Hills Cop: Axel F' Director Mark Molloy Didn't Do Before Taking on Much-Anticipated Fourth Film.* July 1. Accessed October 14, 2024. https://www.indiewire.com/features/interviews/beverly-hills-cop-4-director-mark-molloy-interview-1235021908/.

Feinstein, Howard. 1997. *Metro.* January 18. Accessed November 15, 2024. https://variety.com/1997/film/reviews/metro-1200448423/.

fevercity. n.d. *"Norbit" - 1on1 w/ Eddie Murphy.* Accessed November 17, 2024. https://www.youtube.com/watch?v=Z4wNvkPNP98.

filmSCHOOLarchive. n.d. *Beverly Hills Cop II - Interview.* Accessed October 13, 2024. https://www.youtube.com/watch?v=zo10fukEXiY.

Fisher, Carrie. 1999. *From the Archives: It wasn't in the script: Carrie Fisher interviews Steve Martin about writing.* July 25. Accessed November 2, 2024. https://www.latimes.com/entertainment/movies/moviesnow/la-et-archives-carrie-fisher-steve-martin-interview-19990725-story.html.

Ghosts of Vermont URBEX / Sky's the Limit Videos. n.d. *Daddy Day Care : Good Morning, Eddie Murphy / Quiet on the Set , Special Features (Eddie Murphy).* Accessed November 6, 2024. https://www.youtube.com/watch?v=-goG0RBNe5I.

Gill, Daniel. 2023. *93. THE JOHN LANDIS TAPES, VOL. 5: DIRECTING THE MICHAEL JACKSON "BLACK OR WHITE"*

VIDEO, SYLVESTER STALLONE'S OSCAR, BEVERLY HILLS COP III, THE STUPIDS, AND BLUES BROTHERS 2000. May 12. Accessed October 13, 2024. https://discograffiti.com/podcast/93-the-john-landis-tapes-vol-5-directing-the-michael-jackson-black-or-white-video-sylvester-stallones-oscar-beverly-hills-cop-iii-the-stupids-and-blues-brothers-2000/.

Gillmore, Allson. 2023. *Six cups of hot cocoa.* December 15. Accessed November 2, 2024. https://www.winnipegfreepress.com/arts-and-life/2023/12/15/six-cups-of-hot-cocoa.

Gilmore, Brad. 2022. *Gilbert Gottfriend "Aladdin".* February 22. Accessed October 13, 2024. https://www.spreaker.com/episode/gilbert-gottfried-aladdin--54019828.

Gleiberman, Owen. 2023. *'Candy Cane Lane' Review: Eddie Murphy in a Cozy and Rather Loopy Christmas Movie.* December 3. Accessed November 2, 2024. https://variety.com/2023/film/reviews/candy-cane-lane-review-eddie-murphy-tracee-ellis-ross-1235819573/.

—. 2002. *Showtime.* March 13. Accessed November 17, 2024. https://ew.com/article/2002/03/13/showtime-3/.

Gold Derby. 2016. *Susan McMartin Q&A: 'Mr. Church' writer.* October 2. Accessed November 4, 2024. https://www.goldderby.com/video/susan-mcmartin-qa-mr-church-writer/.

Goldwasser, Dan. 2004. *Interview Harry Gregson-Williams.* 7 5. Accessed 10 30, 2024. https://www.soundtrack.net/content/article/?id=122.

Gonzalez, Ed. 2003. *Review: The Haunted Mansion.* November 22. Accessed October 26, 2024. https://www.slantmagazine.com/film/the-haunted-mansion/.

Gonzalez, Umberto. 2024. *How Will Beall Cracked the 'Beverly Hills Cop: Axel F' Script After 20 Year Development Hell.* July 4. Accessed October 14, 2024. https://www.thewrap.com/will-beall-beverly-hills-cop-axel-f-script/.

Good Morning America. n.d. *Eddie Murphy, Tracee Ellis Ross talk holiday traditions, new film 'Candy Cane Lane'.* Accessed November 2, 2024. https://www.youtube.com/watch?v=w0yyp8G8oYg.

Gordon, Devin. 2011. *The GQA: Brett Ratner.* October 31. Accessed November 17, 2024. https://www.gq.com/story/brett-ratner-director-tower-heist-interview-oscars.

Gore, Chris. 2001. *DR. DOLITTLE 2.* June 24. Accessed October 25, 2024. https://filmthreat.com/uncategorized/dr-dolittle-2/.

Graham, Bob. 1999. *Bowfinger Pokes Hipsters In Hollywood.* August 13. Accessed November 2, 2024. https://www.sfgate.com/movies/article/Bowfinger-Pokes-Hipsters-In-Hollywood-2914582.php.

Grammy Awards. n.d. *Eddie Murphy.* Accessed November 3, 2024. https://www.grammy.com/artists/eddie-murphy/13424.

Guerrasio, Jason. 2017. *The director of classics 'The Warriors' and '48 Hrs.' looks back on his legendary career.* April 9. Accessed October 5, 2024. https://www.businessinsider.com/walter-hill-director-movies-career-2017-4.

Haflidason, Almar. 2000. *Trading Places (1983).* November 17. Accessed November 4, 2024. https://www.bbc.co.uk/films/2000/11/17/trading_places_1983_review.shtml.

Halverson, Mark. 2002. *The Adventures of Pluto Nash.* August 22. Accessed November 17, 2024. https://www.newsreview.com/sacramento/content/the-adventures-of-pluto-nash/12948/.

Harr, Pete Vonder. 2023. *Reviews For The Easily Distracted:.* January 27. Accessed November 4, 2024. https://www.houstonpress.com/arts/things-to-watch-you-people-14956330.

Harris, Blake. 2020. *How Did This Get Made: A Conversation With Ron Underwood, Director Of 'Tremors,' 'City Slickers,' And 'The Adventures Of Pluto Nash'.* July 24. Accessed November 17, 2024. https://www.slashfilm.com/575559/ron-underwood-interview/.

—. 2016. *How Did This Get Made: A Conversation with 'Streets of Fire' Co-Writer Larry Gross.* January 26. Accessed October 5, 2024. https://www.slashfilm.com/542335/streets-of-fire-oral-history/.

Harris, Will. 2020. *Jamie Kennedy Started His Career As A Stand-Up, But Then His Success As An Actor Got In The Way.* June 10. Accessed November 2, 2024. https://decider.com/2020/06/10/jamie-kennedy-interview-stoopid-smart/.

Hass, Lupe R. 2023. *'Candy Cane Lane' Movie Behind the Scenes with Writer Kelly Younger.* December 4. Accessed November 2 , 2024. https://cinemovie.tv/Interviews/Candy-Cane-Lane-Movie-Behind-the-Scenes-with-Writer-Kelly-Younger.

Hiatt, Brian. 2011. *Eddie Murphy Speaks: The Rolling Stone Interview.* November 9. Accessed October 14, 2024. https://www.rollingstone.com/feature/eddie-murphy-speaks-the-rolling-stone-interview-111885/.

HipHollywood. n.d. *Eddie Murphy Talks "A Thousand Words".* Accessed November 6, 2024. https://www.youtube.com/watch?v=UIo0abVrAys.

Historic Films Stock Footage Archive. 2024. *The Nutty Professor II: The Klumps Director Peter Segal Interview Press Junket (2000).* 4 10. Accessed 10 29, 2024. https://www.youtube.com/watch?v=vb39ao2PJ84.

Hollywood Archives. n.d. *'Daddy Day Care' Interview.* Accessed November 6, 2024. https://www.youtube.com/watch?v=V-YOXKB0snY.

Horn, Steven. 2002. *Review of I Spy.* October 31. Accessed November 18, 2024. https://www.ign.com/articles/2002/10/31/review-of-i-spy.

Howe, Desson. 1987. *'Beverly Hills Cop II' .* May 22. Accessed October 13, 2024. https://www.washingtonpost.com/wp-srv/style/longterm/movies/videos/beverlyhillscopiirhowe_a0b0c4.htm.

Hunt, Stacey Wilson. 2016. *Eddie Murphy on Making His First Indie Movie, Celebrating Pluto Nash, and Returning to Stand-up.* December 16. Accessed November 4, 2024. https://www.vulture.com/2016/12/eddie-murphy-mr-church-snl-standup.html.

Igel, Rachel. 2007. *Conversation with a Dream-maker: Bill Condon.* January 1. Accessed November 3, 2024. https://cinemontage.org/bill-condon/.

ingmarlaraTV. n.d. *Norbit-MANY FACES.* Accessed November 17, 2024. https://www.youtube.com/watch?v=tcA7qFbaajc.

itzjakebitch. n.d. *Janet Jackson + Eddie Murphy - Nutty Professor II: The Klumps Interview 2000 (Entertainment Tonight).* Accessed 10 29, 2024. https://www.youtube.com/watch?v=ZzH8Ez4VEHI.

Joe Leydon. n.d. *Eddie Murphy talks to Joe Leydon about "Vampire in Brooklyn".* Accessed November 18, 2024. https://www.youtube.com/watch?v=RDe4PtqKEvk.

Jones, Kimberley. 2022. *Showtime.* March 22. Accessed November 17, 2024. https://www.austinchronicle.com/events/film/2002-03-22/showtime/.

Jones, Tamera. 2023. *Eddie Murphy on 'You People,' Working With Jonah Hill & Returning to 'Beverly Hills Cop'.* January 26. Accessed November 4, 2024. https://collider.com/eddie-murphy-you-people-interview/.

Joseph, André. 2022. *UNFINISHED BUSINESS INTERVIEW – Steven E. de Souza Part 2 (Writer of Street Fighter, Beverly Hills Cop III, & The Flintstones).* October 7. Accessed October 13, 2024. https://ajepyxproductions.com/2022/10/07/unfinished-business-interview-steven-e-de-souza-part-2-writer-of-street-fighter-beverly-hills-cop-iii-the-flintstones/.

Jung, E. Alex. 2020. *In Conversation: Thandie Newton.* July 7. Accessed November 17, 2024. https://www.vulture.com/article/thandie-newton-in-conversation.html.

Kempley, Rita. 2001. *'Dr. Dolittle 2': Gas Menagerie.* June 22. Accessed October 25, 2024. https://www.washingtonpost.com/wp-srv/entertainment/movies/reviews/drdolittle2kempley.htm.

Keough, Peter. 2004. *SHREK 2.* May 21. Accessed October 30, 2004. https://bostonphoenix.com/boston/movies/trailers/documents/03842824.asp.

Kermode, Mark. n.d. *Harlem Nights 1989 .* Accessed November 14, 2024. https://www.timeout.com/movies/harlem-nights.

—. 2007. *Review Shrek the Third.* July 1. Accessed October 31, 2024. https://www.theguardian.com/film/2007/jul/01/animation.family.

Kinowetter. n.d. *Eddie Murphy & Antonio Banderas SHREK 2 (2004) Interview.* Accessed 10 30, 2024. https://www.youtube.com/watch?v=ipfOaCnzUNQ.

Klosterman, Chuck. 1999. *Hollywood skewered.* August 12. Accessed November 2, 2024. https://www.newspapers.com/article/the-akron-beacon-journal-bowfinger/134080346/.

Kluger, Bryan. n.d. *Interview with Thomas Carter on 'When The Game Stands Tall'.* Accessed November 15, 2024. https://www.youtube.com/watch?v=ajuS_S_Gpew.

Korkis, Jim. 2022. *Remembering "Mulan".* August 26. Accessed October 27, 2024. https://cartoonresearch.com/index.php/remembering-mulan/.

Lane, Anthony. 2001. *https://www.newyorker.com/magazine/2001/05/21/fantasy-land.* 5 13. Accessed 10 30, 2020. https://www.newyorker.com/magazine/2001/05/21/fantasy-land.

LaSalle, Mick. 2007. *MOVIE REVIEWS / He can sing, he can dance. But mostly he likes fat suits.* February 9. Accessed November 17, 2024. https://www.sfgate.com/movies/article/MOVIE-REVIEWS-He-can-sing-he-can-dance-But-2618533.php.

Lee, Alana. 2003. *Steve Carr Daddy Day Care.* July 8. Accessed November 6, 2024. https://www.bbc.co.uk/films/2003/07/02/steve_carr_daddy_day_care_interview.shtml.

Leonelli, Elisa. 2023. *Eddie Murphy, 2006 on "Dreamgirls" – Out of the Archives.* January 16. Accessed November 3, 2024. https://goldenglobes.com/articles/eddie-murphy-2006-on-dreamgirls-out-of-the-archives/.

Levinson, Nate. 2015. *Murphy, Wilson Flop in Failed Spy Comedy.* May 1. Accessed November 18, 2024. https://oberlinreview.org/8191/arts/murphy-wilson-flop-in-failed-spy-comedy/.

Levyznin. n.d. *Meet the Cast of Shrek The Third | Poznaj Obsadę Shreka Trzeciego [PL CC].* Accessed October 31, 2024. https://www.youtube.com/watch?v=vFZRNGjJDgk.

Lowry, Brian. 1995. *Vampire in Brooklyn.* October 29. Accessed November 19, 2024. https://variety.com/1995/film/reviews/vampire-in-brooklyn-2-1200443148/.

Lumenick, Lou. 2002. *'PLUTO' TRASH : EDDIE MURPHY IS LOST IN SPACE.* August 17. Accessed November 17, 2024. https://nypost.com/2002/08/17/pluto-trash-eddie-murphy-is-lost-in-space/.

Malcolm, Derek. 1988. *Coming to America/The Runner.* July 28. Accessed October 20 , 2024. https://www.newspapers.com/article/the-guardian-coming-to-americathe-runne/81913871/.

Maltin, Leonard. 2021. *'COMING 2 AMERICA' DELIVERS THE LAUGHS.* March 8. Accessed October 21, 2024. https://leonardmaltin.com/coming-2-america-delivers-the-laughs/.

Mannes, George. 1994. *Eddie Murphy's dangerous ride.* June 10. Accessed October 13, 2024. https://ew.com/article/1994/06/10/eddie-murphys-dangerous-ride/.

Manwaring, Kurt. 2018. *Tony Bancroft Looks Back on Mulan, Donny Osmond.* November 14. Accessed October 27, 2024. https://www.fromthedesk.org/10-questions-tony-bancroft/.

Marchese, David. 2024. *The Interview Eddie Murphy is Ready to Look Back .* June 29. Accessed November 17, 2024. https://www.nytimes.com/2024/06/29/magazine/eddie-murphy-interview.html.

Marks, Scott. 2019. *Dolemite Is My Name: the film of Eddie Murphy's career.* October 24. Accessed November 2, 2024. https://www.sandiegoreader.com/news/2019/oct/24/movie-review-dolemite-my-name-film-eddie-murphy/.

Martinez, Kiko. 2011. *Tower Heist gives Eddie Murphy a comedy vehicle that doesn't crash and burn.* November 8. Accessed November 17, 2024. https://www.sacurrent.com/movies-tv/tower-heist-gives-eddie-murphy-a-comedy-vehicle-that-doesnt-crash-and-burn-2240998.

—. 2021. *Wesley Snipes chats about his scene-stealing character in Coming 2 America, now on DVD.* June 18. Accessed October 21, 2024. https://www.sacurrent.com/movies-tv/wesley-snipes-chats-about-his-scene-stealing-character-in-coming-2-america-now-on-dvd-26465247.

Maslin, Janet. 1984. *FILM: MURPHY IN 'BEVERLY HILLS COP'.* December 5. Accessed October 11, 2024. https://www.nytimes.com/1984/12/05/movies/film-murphy-in-beverly-hills-cop.html.

McClintock, Pamela. 2019. *Netflix Dates 'Marriage Story,' 'Laundromat' and Other Fall Award Films.* August 27. Accessed November 3, 2024. https://www.hollywoodreporter.com/tv/tv-news/netflix-fall-films-marriage-story-laundromat-release-dates-revealed-1234853/.

McDonnell, Brandy. 2009. *Movie Review: 'Imagine That' is unexpectedly engaging.* June 12. Accessed November 15, 2024. https://www.oklahoman.com/story/entertainment/2009/06/12/movie-review-imagine-that-is-unexpectedly-engaging/61395316007/.

McLeod, Mark. 2007. *Interview: Terry Crews of Norbit and The CW's Everybody Hates Chris.* February 7. Accessed November 17, 2024. https://www.showbizmonkeys.com/features.php?id=5.

Media Graveyard. n.d. *Showtime (2002) - The Making of Showtime Featurette.* Accessed November 17, 2024. https://www.youtube.com/watch?v=8ghgziQZt6s.

Morgenstern, Joe. 2004. *Fall in Love All Ogre Again: When Shrek Meets In-Laws, The Honeymoon Is Ours.* May 21. Accessed October 30, 2024. https://www.wsj.com/articles/SB108509699305017631.

Movieclips 101. n.d. *The Haunted Mansion (2003) - Interview With Eddie Murphy.* Accessed October 26, 2024. https://www.youtube.com/watch?v=SEKhzlDgR7c.

Musgrove, James. 2009. *Eddie Murphy: Delirious (25th Anniversary Edition) DVD Review.* May 27. Accessed November 3, 2024. https://www.ign.com/articles/2009/05/27/eddie-murphy-delirious-25th-anniversary-edition-dvd-review.

Nashawaty, Chris. 2011. *Jerry Lewis comedies being remade: Is an overdue revival afoot?* January 18. Accessed October 27, 2024. https://ew.com/article/2011/01/18/jerry-lewis-remakes-2/.

Newcott, Bill. 2019. *Review: Dolemite Is My Name — Movies for the Rest of Us with Bill Newcott.* October 17. Accessed November 2, 2024. https://www.saturdayeveningpost.com/2019/10/review-dolemite-is-my-name-movies-for-the-rest-of-us-with-bill-newcott/.

Nunya Biz. n.d. *Eddie Murphy Received Backlash When He Made Boomerang.* Accessed November 2, 2024. https://www.youtube.com/watch?v=s7zn-RO4ueM.

Original Cin. 2023. *Original-Cin Q&A: Reginald Hudlin - 30 Years Post Boomerang - Reuniting With Eddie Murphy on Candy Cane Lane.* November 27. Accessed November 2, 2024. https://www.original-cin.ca/posts/2023/11/27/original-cin-qampa-reginald-hudlin-30-years-post-boomerang-on-reuniting-with-eddie-murphy-on-candy-cane-lane.

Padilla, Leo. n.d. *12 17 1984 Letterman Eddie Murphy, John Lowe.* Accessed November 17, 2024. https://www.youtube.com/watch?v=48XPt-SxXhU.

Pearlman, Jeff. 2011. *Geoff Rodkey.* May 5. Accessed November 6, 2024. https://jeffpearlman.com/2011/05/05/the-quaz-qa-geoff-rodkey/.

Phillips, David. 2019. *Screenwriters Larry Karaszewski & Scott Alexander On Working With Eddie Murphy And The Long Journey To The Screen Of Dolemite Is My Name.* December 31. Accessed November 2, 2024. https://www.awardsdaily. com/2019/11/screenwriters-larry-karaszewski-scott-alexander-on-working-with-eddie-murphy-and-the-long-journey-to-the-screen-of-dolemite-is-my-name/.

Planet BluRay. n.d. *I Spy Gadgets & GIzmos The Making & Behind the Scenes.* Accessed November 18, 2024. https://www.youtube. com/watch?v=dE-xmbdPNiY.

Planet Money. 2013. *Guy Who Wrote 'Trading Places' Responds To Our Show About His Movie.* July 24. Accessed November 4, 2024. https://www.npr.org/sections/money/2013/07/24/205167911/ guy-who-wrote-trading-places-responds-to-our-show-about-his-movie.

Polowy, Kevin. 2021. *Eddie Murphy explains how Arnold Schwarzenegger inspired 'Coming 2 America'.* March 4. Accessed October 21, 2024. https://www.yahoo.com/entertainment/ coming-2-america-eddie-murphy-arnold-schwarzenegger-terminator-influence-de-aging-arsenio-hall-160049561.html.

Presents, CBR. 2024. *Eddie Murphy Reveals the Secret Reason Behind Beverly Hills Cop's Success.* June 27. Accessed October 14, 2024. https://www.youtube.com/watch?v=GkVWBdy5bNY.

Prigge, Matt. 2023. *The Curious Story Of George Santos Sounds An Awful Lot Like An Old Eddie Murphy Comedy, Says That Film's Co-Writer.* November 28. Accessed November 2, 2024. https:// uproxx.com/viral/george-santos-story-eddie-murphy-film-distinguished-gentleman/.

Pulaski, Steve. 2023. *Best Defense (1984) review.* September 5. Accessed November 17, 2024. https://www.stevepulaski. com/2023/09/05/best-defense-1984-review/.

Put Up Shut Up & Stand Up. n.d. *DOUG WILLIAMS: Working with Eddie Murphy and Dave Chappelle on Nutty Professor.*

Accessed October 27, 2024. https://www.youtube.com/watch?v=YC4_7pHZtfA.

Quinn, Anthony. 2001. *Shrek (U)*. 6 28. Accessed 10 30, 2024. https://www.independent.co.uk/arts-entertainment/films/reviews/shrek-u-9153444.html.

Rabin, Nathan. 2002. *Holy Man.* March 29. Accessed November 15, 2024. https://www.avclub.com/holy-man-1798196047.

—. 2012. *Joe Pantoliano was in Risky Business and The Sopranos and has stories to prove it.* May 3. Accessed November 17, 2024. https://www.avclub.com/joe-pantoliano-was-in-risky-business-and-the-sopranos-a-1798231134.

—. 2012. *Joe Pantoliano was in Risky Business and The Sopranos and has stories to prove it.* May 3. Accessed November 17, 2024. https://www.avclub.com/joe-pantoliano-was-in-risky-business-and-the-sopranos-a-1798231134.

—. 2012. *Random Roles: John Witherspoon.* March 16. Accessed November 18, 2024. https://www.avclub.com/john-witherspoon-1798230387.

Raftery, Brian. 2014. *Mystery Science Theater 3000: The Definitive Oral History of a TV Masterpiece.* April 22. Accessed November 18, 2024. https://www.wired.com/2014/04/mst3k-oral-history/.

Rainer, Peter. 1990. *MOVIE REVIEW : Another 95 Minutes : Sequel: 'Another 48 HRS.,' a crude rehashing of the 1982 hit, reteams Eddie Murphy and Nick Nolte in wall-to-wall mayhem.* June 8. Accessed October 9, 2024. https://www.latimes.com/archives/la-xpm-1990-06-08-ca-784-story.html.

—. 1994. *Movie Reviews: 911 for '90210' Cop .* May 25. Accessed October 13, 2024. https://www.latimes.com/archives/la-xpm-1994-05-25-ca-61972-story.html.

Ranier, Peter. 2000. *In Brief: 'Coyote Ugly' and 'Nutty Professor II: The Klumps'.* 8 14. Accessed 10 29, 2024. https://nymag.com/nymetro/movies/reviews/3642/.

Red Carpet Report on Mingle Media TV. n.d. *Director, Bruce Beresford interviewed at the Red Carpet Premiere of Mr. Church.* Accessed November 4, 2024. https://www.youtube.com/watch?v=joRJTTd0TiI.

Rich, Jamie S. 2007. *Eddie Murphy - Delirious.* February 6. Accessed November 3, 2024. https://www.dvdtalk.com/reviews/26512/eddie-murphy-delirious/.

Rodriguez, Karla. 2023. *Sam Jays Calls Working Alongside Jonah Hill in 'You People' a 'Dream Come True'.* January 27. Accessed November 4, 2024. https://www.complex.com/pop-culture/a/karla-rodriguez/sam-jay-makes-film-debut-in-you-people-interview.

Rogers, Nick. 2006. *Dreamgirls.* December 22. Accessed November 3, 2024. https://midwestfilmjournal.com/2006/12/22/dreamgirls/.

Rosenbaum, Jonathan. 1985. *Another 48 Hrs. - The Chicago Reader.* October 26. Accessed October 9, 2024. https://chicagoreader.com/film/another-48-hrs/.

—. n.d. *Boomerang.* Accessed November 2024, 2024. https://chicagoreader.com/film/boomerang-5/.

Rowlands, Paul. 2012. *DANIEL PETRIE JR ON 'BEVERLY HILLS COP'.* September. Accessed October 11, 2024. https://www.money-into-light.com/2012/09/daniel-petrie-jr-on-beverly-hills-cop.html.

Rubin, Sylvia. 1996. *PAGE ONE -- After 15 Years, Actor Apologizes For Gay Slurs.* May 11. Accessed November 3, 2024. https://www.sfgate.com/news/article/PAGE-ONE-After-15-Years-Actor-Apologizes-For-2982557.php.

Ruby, Ayla. 2023. *Exclusive: Interview with 'Candy Cane Lane' Director Reginald Hudlin.* November 30. Accessed November 2, 2024. https://thecosmiccircus.com/exclusive-interview-with-candy-cane-lane-director-reginald-hudlin/.

Russian, Ale. 2020. *Coming 2 America First Look: James Earl Jones Says It's 'the Perfect Time' to 'Return to Zamunda!'.* December

17. Accessed October 20, 2024. https://www.yahoo.com/entertainment/coming-2-america-first-look-150031365.html.

Ryan, Desmond. 1982. *48 Hrs. Philadelphia Inquirer review - Newspapers.com.* December 10. Accessed October 24, 2024. https://www.newspapers.com/article/the-philadelphia-inquirer-48-hrs-philad/121932768/.

SBS. 2009. *Daddy Day Care Review.* January 1. Accessed November 6, 2024. https://www.sbs.com.au/whats-on/article/daddy-day-care-review/jf79gfw3w.

Scheck, Frank. 2016. *'Mr. Church': Tribeca Review.* April 22. Accessed November 4, 2024. https://www.hollywoodreporter.com/news/general-news/mr-church-tribeca-review-887130/.

Schickel, Richard. 1994. *CINEMA: Eddie Who?* June 6. Accessed October 13, 2024. https://time.com/archive/6725416/cinema-eddie-who/.

Schwarzbaum, Lisa. 1998. *Dr. Dolittle.* July 10. Accessed October 25, 2024. https://ew.com/article/1998/07/10/dr-dolittle-3/.

—. 1998. *Holy Man.* October 16. Accessed November 15, 2024. https://ew.com/article/1998/10/16/holy-man-2/.

ScreenSlam. n.d. *Imagine That: Eddie Murphy & Yara Shahidi Interview | ScreenSlam.* Accessed November 15, 2024. https://www.youtube.com/watch?v=-uVqMizr6Fs.

Seitz, Loree. 2024. *Eddie Murphy's 'Beverly Hills Cop: Axel F' Debuts as Most-Watched Netflix Title of the Week With 41 Million Views.* July 9. Accessed October 20, 2024. https://www.thewrap.com/beverly-hills-cop-axel-f-netflix-viewership/.

Sheehan, Henry. 1988. *Little Boy Blue.* January 21. Accessed November 3, 2024. https://chicagoreader.com/film/little-boy-blue-2/.

—. 1987. *Runaway Vehicle.* May 28. Accessed October 13 , 2024. https://chicagoreader.com/film/runaway-vehicle/.

Show Master. n.d. *Coming to America- An interview with Eddie Murphy and Arsenio Hall.* Accessed October 20, 2024. https://www.youtube.com/watch?v=YxZZlFuAr_s.

Simonpillai, Radheyan. 2021. *What's new to VOD and streaming this weekend.* March 5. Accessed October 21, 2024. https://nowtoronto.com/movies/whats-new-to-streaming-vod-canada-this-weekend-march-5-7-2021/.

Simpsons, MJ. 2015. *interview: Lane Smith.* March 10. Accessed November 2, 2024. https://mjsimpson-films.blogspot.com/2015/03/interview-lane-smith.html.

Sinclair, Tom. 1999. *Wyclef Jean writes music for "Life".* January 22. Accessed November 3, 2024. https://ew.com/article/1999/01/22/wyclef-jean-writes-music-life/.

Singer, Matt. 2021. *I was really inspired by Fiddler on the Roof. It's one of my favorite musicals. And I love the idea of a person who is entrenched in traditions for the right reasons suddenly realizing that the world is changing. And it's also affecting the people that he.* March 4. Accessed October 21, 2024. https://screencrush.com/craig-brewer-interview-coming-2-america/.

Soto, Sophia. n.d. *Judge Reinhold and John Ashton on Returning for 'Beverly Hills Cop: Axel F'.* Accessed October 20, 2024. https://thenerdsofcolor.org/2024/07/09/judge-reinhold-and-john-ashton-on-returning-for-beverly-hills-cop-axel-f/.

Spin Magazine. 2020. *Eddie Murphy and Spike Lee in Conversation: Our 1990 Cover Story.* October. Accessed November 14, 2024. https://www.spin.com/2020/11/eddie-murphy-and-spike-lee-in-conversation-our-1990-cover-story/.

Stack, Peter. 1998. *Disney Gives Animated 'Mulan' a Deft Human Touch.* June 19. Accessed October 27, 2024. https://www.sfgate.com/movies/article/Disney-Gives-Animated-Mulan-a-Deft-Human-Touch-3003722.php.

Staff, EW. 2001. *Dr. Dolittle 2.* April 20. Accessed October 25, 2024. https://ew.com/article/2001/04/20/dr-dolittle-2/.

—. 2000. *NUTTY PROFESSOR II: THE KLUMPS.* April 28. Accessed 10 29, 2024. https://ew.com/article/2000/04/28/nutty-professor-ii-klumps-5/.

Sterritt, David. 1999. *Terrific duo finds comedy in doing 'Life'*. April 16. Accessed November 3, 2024. https://www.csmonitor.com/1999/0416/p15s2.html.

Steve, Ryfle, and Den Shewman. 2016. *Ted Elliott and Terry Rossio on Shrek.* 6 9. Accessed 10 30, 2024. https://www.creativescreenwriting.com/shrek-5/.

steve6231. n.d. *Beverly Hills Cop 2: (The Phenomenon Continues).* Accessed October 13, 2024. https://www.youtube.com/watch?v=kzyfPknXc1M.

Stevens, Dana. 2006. *Sugar and Spice The schlocky appeal of Dreamgirls.* December 21. Accessed November 3, 2024. https://slate.com/culture/2006/12/the-schlocky-appeal-of-dreamgirls.html.

Swann, Erik. 2013. *Why Eddie Murphy's Beverly Hills Cop TV Pilot Didn't Move Forward At CBS, According To The EP.* April 1. Accessed October 14, 2024. https://www.cinemablend.com/interviews/why-eddie-murphys-beverly-hills-cop-tv-pilot-didnt-move-forward-at-cbs-according-to-the-ep.

take2markTV. n.d. *Rewind: Eddie Murphy on making "Dr. Dolittle" & challenging animal actors (1998).* Accessed October 21, 2024. https://www.youtube.com/watch?v=0inpAGj48FE.

Talk Shows. n.d. *[Talk Shows]Eddie Murphy Stand Up, Oscars, SNL and alot more crazy stuff with Jimmy Fallon.* Accessed November 15, 2024. https://www.youtube.com/watch?v=mHuhWRRn9ds.

Tangcay, Jazz. 2020. *How 'Dolemite Is My Name' Editor Billy Fox Balanced Comedy-Drama Pacing.* January 2. Accessed November 2, 2024. https://variety.com/2020/artisans/awards/dolemite-is-my-name-editing-billy-fox-1203455302/.

Taylor, Drew. 2024. *'Kung Fu Panda 4' Director Mike Mitchell on His Big Return to DreamWorks: 'It Is a Completely Different Studio'.* April 10. Accessed October 31, 2024. https://www.thewrap.com/kung-fu-panda-4-mike-mitchell-shrek-interview/.

Television Academy Foundation. n.d. *Keenen Ivory Wayans Performer/Producer/Show Creator.* Accessed November 3, 2024. https://interviews.televisionacademy.com/interviews/keenen-ivory-wayans.

Tellado, Tony. 1998. *BladeZone Presents: Brion James Interview from 1998.* September. Accessed October 9, 2024. https://media.bladezone.com/contents/film/interviews/brion-james/.

That's Entertainment. n.d. *Eddie Murphy 1994 Australia Interview.* Accessed October 13, 2024. https://www.youtube.com/watch?v=8LRVchGq2lo.

The Bobbie Wygant Archive. 1998. *Betty Thomas "Dr. Dolittle" 6/7/98 - Bobbie Wygant Archive.* June 7. Accessed October 21, 2024. https://www.youtube.com/watch?v=tNK0uUSUSRw.

—. n.d. *Dudley Moore for "Unfaithfully Yours" 1984 - Bobbie Wygant Archive.* Accessed November 17, 2024. https://www.youtube.com/watch?v=udeXnWRbZeM.

The Bobby Wygant Archive. n.d. *Nick Nolte for "48 Hrs" 1982 - Bobbie Wygant Archive.* Accessed October 7, 2024. https://www.youtube.com/watch?v=97kNPwsM8iE.

The Independent. 2019. *Eddie Murphy: 'I was kind of an a**hole'.* October 14. Accessed November 2, 2024. https://www.the-independent.com/arts-entertainment/films/features/eddie-murphy-interview-dolemite-is-my-name-netflix-saturday-night-live-comedy-a9148896.html.

The Julie Andrews Archive. n.d. *(Short) Behind the Scenes of Shrek 2 (2004) - Julie Andrews, John Cleese.* Accessed 10 30, 2024. https://www.youtube.com/watch?v=RziodA1Npsc.

The Washington Post. 2015. *They played here.* February 27. Accessed November 3, 2024. https://www.washingtonpost.com/entertainment/they-played-here/2015/02/26/d59b5514-b926-11e4-9423-f3d0a1ec335c_story.html.

TheCelebFactor. 2011. *Ben Stiller and Eddie Murphy Tower Heist interview.* November 8. Accessed November 17, 2024. https://www.youtube.com/watch?v=99-CJvYOXUU.

TheHumorMill. n.d. *EXCLUSIVE- On Set Of The New Beverly Hills Cop TV Show With Brandon T Jackson.* Accessed October 14, 2024. https://www.youtube.com/watch?v=HnKmUWmxSsw.

Thomas, Kevin. 1984. *48. Hrs. Los Angeles Times review - Newspapers. com.* December 9. Accessed October 9, 2024. https://www.newspapers.com/article/the-los-angeles-times-48-hrs-los-angele/121932872/.

Thompson, Anne. 1990. *EW finds out how "48 More Hours" came together.* June 22. Accessed October 9, 2024. https://ew.com/article/1990/06/22/ew-finds-out-how-48-more-hours-came-together/.

Thompson, Homer. n.d. *Life (1999) Rick Baker Makeup Featurette.* Accessed November 3, 2024. https://www.youtube.com/watch?v=-0DsGmVbPyU.

—. n.d. *The Making of Life (1999) Featurette.* Accessed November 3, 2024. https://www.youtube.com/watch?v=lkOBmI_86jM.

Thompson, Simon. 2024. *Composing The 'Beverly Hills Cop: Axel F' Score Was Fate For Lorne Balfe.* July 10. Accessed October 20, 2024. https://www.forbes.com/sites/simonthompson/2024/07/10/composing-the-beverly-hills-cop-4-score-was-fate-for-lorne-balfe/.

—. 2023. *Why Kenya Barris Wanted 'You People' To Be His Feature Directorial Debut.* January 27. Accessed November 4, 2024. https://www.forbes.com/sites/simonthompson/2023/01/27/why-kenya-barris-wanted-you-people-to-be-his-feature-directorial-debut/.

Tobias, Adam. 2008. *'Meet Dave' is out of this world bad.* July 11. Accessed November 18, 2024. https://www.wdtimes.com/features/screen_scenes/meet-dave-is-out-of-this-world-bad/article_485ef00a-5aec-5dc3-a071-c6745defafa9.html.

Travers, Peter. 2024. *Review: To see Murphy, Reinhold and Ashton mix it up again in 'Beverly Hills Cop 4', is fine fan service.* July 3. Accessed October 20, 2024. https://abcnews.go.com/GMA/Culture/review-murphy-reinhold-ashton-mix-beverly-hills-cop/story?id=111579853.

—. 2010. *Shrek Forever After.* May 20. Accessed November 2, 2024. https://www.rollingstone.com/tv-movies/tv-movie-reviews/shrek-forever-after-125926/.

Tuckey, Tammy. 2023. *"The Haunted Mansion" (2003) Cast & Crew Reunion.* October 14. Accessed October 26, 2024. https://tammytuckey.com/whats-new/the-haunted-mansion-2003-cast-amp-crew-reunion.

TV Guide. 2002. *Pluto Nash Soundbite: Rosario Dawson On Her Character.* August 15. Accessed November 17, 2024. https://www.tvguide.com/videos/the-adventures-of-pluto-nash/2030283109/pluto-nash-soundbite-rosario-dawson-on-her-character/3558443/.

Tyler, Josh. 2016. *Meet Dave.* May 27. Accessed November 18, 2024. https://www.cinemablend.com/reviews/Meet-Dave-3234.html.

VHS Video Vault. n.d. *Clive Anderson interviews Eddie Murphy.* Accessed October 27, 2024. https://www.youtube.com/watch?v=J2tQdsVhOUc.

Vincent, Mal. 1995. *WES CRAVEN NOT WHAT YOU'D EXPECT.* October 30. Accessed November 18, 2024. https://scholar.lib.vt.edu/VA-news/VA-Pilot/issues/1995/vp951030/10280055.htm.

Weintraub, Steven. 2010. *Mike Myers, Cameron Diaz, Eddie Murphy, Antonio Banderas and Ryan Seacrest Interview SHREK FOREVER AFTER.* May 19. Accessed October 31, 2024. https://collider.com/shrek-forever-after-interview-mike-myers-cameron-diaz-eddie-murphy-antonio-banderas-jon-hamm-craig-robinson-ryan-seacrest/.

WFAA. n.d. *John Lithgow says he was almost the voice of Hades in Hercules while talking about being in Shrek.* Accessed 10 30, 2024. https://www.youtube.com/watch?v=zQn-Ljm6gHU.

Wilson, Jake. 2009. *Show me the funny money.* September 17. Accessed November 15, 2024. https://www.theage.com.au/entertainment/movies/show-me-the-funny-money-20090917-ge83jo.html.

Wolff, Ellen. 2008. *Mark Stetson Steps Up To 'Meet Dave'.* July 10. Accessed November 18, 2024. https://www.awn.com/vfxworld/mark-stetson-steps-meet-dave.

Woodroof, Cory. 2024. *Ranking the 10 greatest Eddie Murphy film performances, including Axel Foley.* July 8. Accessed October 27, 2024. https://ftw.usatoday.com/lists/10-greatest-eddie-murphy-film-performances-axel-foley.

Zehme, Bill. 1989. *Eddie Murphy: Call Him Money.* August 24. Accessed November 3, 2024. https://web.archive.org/web/20180712154245/https://www.rollingstone.com/culture/culture-news/eddie-murphy-call-him-money-82359/.

Zemler, Emily. 2016. *Charles Dance takes a look back at some of his biggest roles.* June 3. Accessed November 3, 2024. https://www.latimes.com/entertainment/movies/la-ca-mn-charles-dance-imdb-20160528-snap-story.html.

Zinoman, Jason. 2019. *Eddie Murphy Is Bringing Eddie Murphy Back.* September 26. Accessed November 3, 2024. https://www.nytimes.com/2019/09/26/movies/eddie-murphy.html.